ADHD

10 Strategies to Succeed with ADHD

A comprehensive guide designed to help individuals with Attention-Deficit/Hyperactivity Disorder (ADHD) navigate the challenges they face and achieve success in various aspects of their lives. The book is divided into 10 chapters, each representing one strategy, and further broken down into five subchapters to provide a deep understanding of each approach. The strategies covered in this book are grounded in scientific research, personal experiences, and expert advice, providing a holistic approach to managing ADHD and unlocking one's full potential.

Chapter 1: Understanding ADHD

1.1. The Science Behind ADHD

Attention-Deficit/Hyperactivity Disorder (ADHD) is a neurodevelopmental disorder that affects both children and adults. It is characterized by a pattern of inattention, impulsivity, and hyperactivity that can interfere with everyday functioning and development. In this section, we will explore the scientific foundation of ADHD, including its neurological basis, genetic factors, and environmental influences.

Neurological Basis:

ADHD is associated with differences in brain structure and function. Research has shown that individuals with ADHD tend to have a smaller prefrontal cortex, a region responsible for executive functions such as attention, decision-making, and impulse control. Additionally, the brain's neurotransmitter systems, particularly dopamine and norepinephrine, are believed to play a crucial role in the development and manifestation of ADHD symptoms. Imbalances in these neurotransmitters can lead to difficulties in maintaining attention, regulating emotions, and controlling impulses.

Genetic Factors:

ADHD has a strong genetic component, with studies estimating that heritability accounts for 70-80% of the disorder. This means that if a parent or sibling has ADHD, there is a higher likelihood of another family member being diagnosed with the condition. Researchers have identified several genes that are associated with ADHD, many of which are involved in the regulation of neurotransmitters, brain development, and synaptic connections. However, it is essential to note that no single gene causes ADHD, and it is likely that multiple genes contribute to the disorder.

Environmental Influences:

While genetics play a significant role in the development of ADHD, environmental factors can also contribute to the onset and severity of symptoms. Prenatal factors, such as maternal smoking, alcohol use, and exposure to toxins, have been associated with an increased risk of ADHD in children. Additionally, adverse childhood experiences, including trauma, abuse, and neglect, can exacerbate ADHD symptoms and complicate the disorder's management. It is crucial to consider both genetic and environmental influences when addressing ADHD to provide the most effective interventions and support.

In summary, the science behind ADHD is complex and multifaceted. The disorder is rooted in neurological differences, genetic predispositions, and environmental factors, all of which contribute to the development and manifestation of symptoms. Understanding the scientific basis of ADHD is essential in providing accurate information, raising awareness, and guiding effective treatment strategies for individuals living with the condition.

1.2. Common Symptoms and Types of ADHD

ADHD manifests in various symptoms that can be grouped into three primary categories: inattention, hyperactivity, and impulsivity. While the symptoms may differ from person to person, they typically cause significant impairments in daily functioning. In this section, we will explore the common symptoms associated with each category and discuss the three types of ADHD.

Inattention:

Symptoms of inattention may include:

1. Difficulty sustaining attention in tasks or activities

2. Frequent careless mistakes in schoolwork, work, or other activities

3. Trouble organizing tasks and activities

4. Easily distracted by external stimuli or unrelated thoughts

5. Forgetfulness in daily activities

6. Avoidance or reluctance to engage in tasks that require sustained mental effort

7. Frequently losing items necessary for tasks or activities

Hyperactivity:

Symptoms of hyperactivity may include:

1. Excessive fidgeting, tapping, or squirming in one's seat

2. Difficulty staying seated in situations where it is

expected

3. Inability to engage in leisure activities quietly

4. Excessive talking or interrupting others

5. Always seeming to be "on the go" or "driven by a motor"

6. Running or climbing in inappropriate situations

Impulsivity:

Symptoms of impulsivity may include:

1. Blurting out answers before questions have been completed

2. Difficulty waiting for one's turn in conversations or activities

3. Interrupting or intruding on others' activities

4. Acting without considering the consequences of actions

5. Making decisions hastily without sufficient reflection

Types of ADHD:

Based on the predominant symptoms, ADHD can be classified into three types:

1. Predominantly Inattentive Presentation (ADHD-PI): This type is characterized by significant inattention symptoms with few or no symptoms of hyperactivity-impulsivity. Individuals with ADHD-PI may have difficulty staying focused on tasks, following instructions, and organizing activities.

2. Predominantly Hyperactive-Impulsive Presentation

(ADHD-PH): This type is characterized by significant hyperactivity-impulsivity symptoms with few or no symptoms of inattention. Individuals with ADHD-PH may struggle with impulsivity, excessive talking, and constantly being in motion.

3. Combined Presentation (ADHD-C): This type includes a combination of inattention and hyperactivity-impulsivity symptoms. Individuals with ADHD-C exhibit significant difficulties in both categories and often require a comprehensive approach to managing their symptoms.

In conclusion, ADHD is a complex disorder that presents with various symptoms related to inattention, hyperactivity, and impulsivity. Understanding the common symptoms and different types of ADHD is crucial for accurate diagnosis, effective treatment planning, and tailored support for individuals living with the condition.

1.3. The Impact of ADHD on Daily Life

ADHD can significantly impact various aspects of daily life, including academic performance, work productivity, social relationships, and overall well-being. In this section, we will discuss the potential challenges individuals with ADHD may face in different areas of their lives and the importance of addressing these issues through appropriate interventions and support.

Academic Performance:

Children and adolescents with ADHD often struggle in school due to difficulties with attention, organization, and impulse control. They may have trouble staying focused during lessons, completing assignments on time, and following instructions. As a result, they might experience lower academic achievement, increased rates of grade retention, and higher dropout rates compared to their peers without ADHD.

Work Productivity:

Adults with ADHD may face challenges in the workplace due to similar issues with attention, organization, and impulsivity. They might struggle to meet deadlines, manage multiple tasks, or maintain focus during meetings. These challenges can result in decreased work performance, difficulties in career advancement, and increased job turnover. Moreover, adults with undiagnosed or untreated ADHD may experience a heightened sense of frustration, stress, and low self-esteem related to their work performance.

Social Relationships:

ADHD can also affect social relationships for individuals of all ages. Impulsivity and hyperactivity may lead to interruptions in conversations, difficulty waiting for one's turn, or acting inappropriately in social situations. These behaviors can create challenges in forming and maintaining friendships, romantic relationships, and family connections. Furthermore, individuals with ADHD may feel misunderstood or judged by others, leading to feelings of isolation and loneliness.

Emotional Well-being:

Living with ADHD can take an emotional toll, as individuals may experience increased stress, anxiety, and frustration due to their symptoms. They may have difficulty regulating emotions and coping with daily challenges, leading to mood swings and emotional outbursts. In some cases, individuals with ADHD may also develop coexisting mental health conditions, such as anxiety, depression, or substance abuse disorders, which can further complicate their emotional well-being.

In summary, ADHD can have a profound impact on various aspects of daily life, including academic performance, work productivity, social relationships, and emotional well-being. It is essential to recognize the challenges individuals with ADHD may face and provide appropriate interventions, accommodations, and support to help them succeed and thrive in their personal and professional lives.

1.4. The Importance of Early Diagnosis

Early diagnosis of ADHD is crucial for several reasons, as it can significantly improve the individual's overall quality of life, academic and work success, and emotional well-being. In this section, we will discuss the benefits of early diagnosis and the potential consequences of delayed or missed diagnosis.

Benefits of Early Diagnosis:

1. Timely intervention: Early diagnosis enables individuals with ADHD to receive appropriate interventions and support as soon as possible. This may include behavioral therapies, academic accommodations, medication, or a combination of these strategies. Early intervention can help individuals manage their symptoms more effectively, leading to better outcomes in various aspects of their lives.

2. Improved academic performance: Diagnosing and treating ADHD early can help children and adolescents perform better in school by addressing attention, organization, and impulse control issues. With the right support and accommodations in place, students with ADHD are more likely to reach their full academic potential.

3. Enhanced social relationships: Early diagnosis and intervention can help individuals with ADHD develop better social skills, enabling them to form and maintain meaningful relationships with peers, family members, and romantic partners. Addressing impulsivity and hyperactivity symptoms can lead to improved communication and social interactions.

4. Better emotional well-being: Early diagnosis of ADHD allows individuals to better understand their symptoms and develop effective coping strategies for managing daily challenges. As a result, they may experience reduced stress, anxiety, and frustration, leading to improved emotional well-being and mental health.

5. Prevention of secondary issues: Identifying and addressing ADHD early on can help prevent the development of secondary problems, such as low self-esteem, anxiety, depression, or substance abuse disorders. By addressing the primary symptoms of ADHD, individuals may be less likely to develop these coexisting conditions.

Consequences of Delayed or Missed Diagnosis:

1. Academic struggles: Without early diagnosis and intervention, children and adolescents with ADHD may continue to struggle in school, resulting in lower academic achievement, grade retention, or dropping out.

2. Work difficulties: Undiagnosed or untreated ADHD in adults can lead to decreased work performance, job dissatisfaction, and increased job turnover.

3. Strained relationships: Delayed diagnosis can result in ongoing challenges in forming and maintaining social relationships, leading to feelings of isolation and loneliness.

4. Compromised emotional well-being: Individuals with undiagnosed or untreated ADHD may experience

increased stress, anxiety, and frustration, potentially leading to the development of coexisting mental health conditions.

In conclusion, early diagnosis of ADHD is essential for ensuring timely intervention, improved academic and work success, and better emotional well-being. By identifying and addressing ADHD symptoms as early as possible, individuals can receive the necessary support and accommodations to help them thrive in their personal and professional lives.

1.5. Myths and Misconceptions about ADHD

Despite growing awareness and understanding of ADHD, there are still numerous myths and misconceptions surrounding the disorder. These inaccuracies can contribute to stigma, misunderstandings, and barriers to appropriate care and support. In this section, we will address some common myths and misconceptions about ADHD and provide accurate information to counter them.

Myth 1: ADHD is not a real disorder.

Fact: ADHD is a well-established neurodevelopmental disorder recognized by major medical organizations, including the American Psychiatric Association and the World Health Organization. Decades of scientific research have demonstrated that ADHD is associated with differences in brain structure, function, and neurotransmitter levels, leading to the characteristic symptoms of inattention, hyperactivity, and impulsivity.

Myth 2: ADHD is caused by poor parenting or a lack of discipline.

Fact: While parenting styles and environmental factors can influence the severity and expression of ADHD symptoms, they are not the primary cause of the disorder. ADHD has a strong genetic component, with heritability estimates ranging from 70-80%. Parenting and environmental factors can play a role in managing ADHD symptoms, but they cannot cause or cure the disorder.

Myth 3: Only children can have ADHD.

Fact: Although ADHD is often diagnosed in childhood, the disorder can persist into adulthood. It is estimated that around 50-60% of children with ADHD continue to experience significant symptoms as adults. In some cases, individuals may not be diagnosed with ADHD until adulthood, as their symptoms may have been less apparent or misattributed to other causes in childhood.

Myth 4: People with ADHD are just lazy or unintelligent.

Fact: ADHD is not related to a person's intelligence or motivation. Individuals with ADHD can be highly intelligent and successful in various fields. However, they may struggle with specific challenges related to attention, organization, and impulse control, which can make certain tasks more difficult. With the right support and accommodations, people with ADHD can thrive academically and professionally.

Myth 5: Medication is the only treatment option for ADHD.

Fact: While medication can be an effective treatment for many individuals with ADHD, it is not the only option. Behavioral therapies, such as cognitive-behavioral therapy (CBT) and parent training, can also be helpful in managing ADHD symptoms. Additionally, lifestyle modifications, such as exercise, sleep hygiene, and nutrition, can play a crucial role in supporting overall well-being and symptom management. The best treatment approach for ADHD is often multimodal, incorporating medication, therapy, and lifestyle changes as needed.

In conclusion, debunking myths and misconceptions about ADHD is vital for promoting understanding, reducing stigma, and ensuring that individuals with the disorder receive the appropriate support and care they need. By providing accurate information about ADHD, we can create a more inclusive and empathetic society for those living with the condition.

Chapter 2: Acceptance and Self-Compassion

2.1. Embracing Your ADHD

Accepting and embracing your ADHD is a crucial step towards managing the condition effectively and living a fulfilling life. This process involves recognizing that ADHD is a part of who you are, understanding its impact on your life, and cultivating self-compassion. In this section, we will discuss strategies for embracing your ADHD and fostering a positive relationship with yourself.

1. Educate yourself: Understanding the nature of ADHD, its symptoms, and its effects on your life can help you accept the condition as a part of your identity. Knowledge can empower you to make informed decisions about your treatment and support, and also help you explain ADHD to others in your life.

2. Focus on strengths: Individuals with ADHD often possess unique strengths and talents, such as creativity, problem-solving, and adaptability. Recognizing and celebrating these strengths can help you develop a more balanced and positive self-image, fostering self-acceptance and self-compassion.

3. Seek support: Connecting with others who have ADHD, such as through support groups or online forums, can provide you with valuable insights, encouragement, and a sense of belonging. Sharing your experiences with others who understand your challenges can help you feel less isolated and more accepting of your ADHD.

4. Practice self-compassion: It is essential to treat yourself with kindness, understanding, and patience, especially when you face challenges related to ADHD. Acknowledge that living with ADHD can be difficult and that everyone makes mistakes. Instead of criticizing yourself, focus on what you can learn from challenging situations and how you can grow and improve.

5. Set realistic expectations: Accepting your ADHD means acknowledging that certain tasks or situations may be more challenging for you than for others. Adjust your expectations to be realistic and achievable, and celebrate your progress and accomplishments, no matter how small they may seem.

6. Develop coping strategies: Embracing your ADHD involves finding effective ways to manage its impact on your life. Identify strategies that work best for you, such as using a planner to stay organized, setting reminders for appointments, or breaking tasks into smaller steps. Tailor these strategies to your specific needs and preferences.

7. Advocate for yourself: Accepting your ADHD means standing up for yourself and your needs. This may involve requesting accommodations at school or work, educating others about ADHD, or seeking professional help when needed.

In conclusion, embracing your ADHD is an essential step towards self-acceptance and self-compassion. By understanding the nature of the disorder, focusing on your strengths, seeking support, and practicing self-compassion, you can cultivate a positive relationship with yourself and successfully navigate the challenges that ADHD may present in your life.

2.2. Practicing Self-Compassion

Practicing self-compassion is essential for individuals with ADHD, as it helps to cultivate a healthy and supportive relationship with oneself. Self-compassion involves treating oneself with kindness, understanding, and patience, especially when facing challenges or setbacks related to ADHD. In this section, we will discuss strategies for developing self-compassion and incorporating it into your daily life.

1. Mindful awareness: Begin by noticing your self-critical thoughts and feelings when they arise. Pay attention to the language you use with yourself, and observe these thoughts without judgment. Becoming aware of your self-critical tendencies is the first step towards developing self-compassion.

2. Reframe negative self-talk: When you notice negative self-talk, try to reframe it with kinder, more supportive language. For example, instead of telling yourself, "I always mess up," try saying, "I'm doing my best, and it's okay to make mistakes." Remind yourself that nobody is perfect and that everyone faces challenges and setbacks.

3. Practice self-kindness: Treat yourself with the same kindness, understanding, and patience that you would offer to a close friend or family member. Recognize that it's okay to feel frustrated or overwhelmed at times and that these feelings do not define your worth as a person. Offer yourself comfort and support during challenging moments.

4. Embrace imperfection: Understand that everyone has strengths and weaknesses, and nobody is perfect. Instead

of striving for perfection, focus on personal growth and improvement. Recognize your achievements and progress, no matter how small, and remember that your worth is not determined solely by your successes or failures.

5. Develop a self-compassion mantra: Create a personal mantra or affirmation that you can repeat to yourself during difficult moments or when self-critical thoughts arise. This mantra should be positive, supportive, and encouraging. Examples include, "I am enough," "I am doing my best," or "I am worthy of love and kindness."

6. Practice self-care: Taking care of your physical, mental, and emotional well-being is an important aspect of self-compassion. Ensure that you are getting adequate sleep, eating a balanced diet, engaging in regular exercise, and participating in activities that bring you joy and relaxation.

7. Connect with others: Sharing your experiences, challenges, and feelings with supportive friends, family members, or support groups can help foster self-compassion. Connecting with others who understand and empathize with your journey can remind you that you are not alone and that your feelings and experiences are valid.

In conclusion, practicing self-compassion is an essential component of living well with ADHD. By developing mindful awareness, reframing negative self-talk, practicing self-kindness, and connecting with others, you can create a supportive and nurturing relationship with yourself, better navigate the challenges of ADHD, and improve your overall well-being.

2.3. Recognizing Your Strengths and Talents

Individuals with ADHD often possess unique strengths and talents that can be overshadowed by the challenges they face. Recognizing and celebrating these strengths can help build self-confidence, foster self-compassion, and contribute to a more balanced self-image. In this section, we will discuss strategies for identifying your strengths and talents and incorporating them into your daily life.

1. Self-reflection: Take some time to reflect on your personal qualities, skills, and abilities that you believe are your strengths. Consider moments when you have felt successful, proud, or fulfilled, and think about the attributes that contributed to those experiences. You can also ask trusted friends, family members, or colleagues for their perspectives on your strengths.

2. Keep a strengths journal: Document your strengths and talents by maintaining a journal where you can record your achievements, positive feedback from others, and moments when you have utilized your strengths effectively. Reviewing this journal regularly can help reinforce your self-confidence and remind you of your capabilities.

3. Set goals that align with your strengths: Identify goals that are aligned with your strengths and talents. Focusing on tasks and activities that utilize your unique abilities can increase your motivation, sense of accomplishment, and overall satisfaction.

4. Seek opportunities to showcase your talents: Look for opportunities to demonstrate and develop your strengths,

both personally and professionally. This might involve joining clubs, volunteering, or taking on projects at work that allow you to use and refine your unique skills.

5. Develop new skills and talents: It's never too late to learn and grow. Pursue interests or hobbies that excite you and provide opportunities to develop new skills. Expanding your skillset can contribute to increased self-confidence and a more diverse range of strengths.

6. Celebrate your successes: Acknowledge and celebrate your achievements, no matter how small they may seem. Recognizing your accomplishments can reinforce your self-confidence and remind you of your unique strengths and talents.

7. Share your strengths with others: Helping others by sharing your strengths and talents can be a fulfilling and empowering experience. Offer your expertise or assistance to friends, family members, or colleagues, and take pride in the positive impact you can make on their lives.

In conclusion, recognizing your strengths and talents is an essential aspect of living well with ADHD. By engaging in self-reflection, setting goals that align with your strengths, and seeking opportunities to showcase and develop your talents, you can foster self-compassion, build self-confidence, and create a more balanced and positive self-image.

2.4. Building a Positive Self-Image

A positive self-image is essential for individuals with ADHD, as it can help boost self-confidence, self-compassion, and overall well-being. Developing a positive self-image involves focusing on your strengths, embracing your unique qualities, and treating yourself with kindness and understanding. In this section, we will discuss strategies for building a positive self-image when living with ADHD.

1. Emphasize your strengths: As discussed in the previous section, recognizing and celebrating your strengths and talents is crucial in developing a positive self-image. Focus on your unique abilities and qualities, and remind yourself of your accomplishments regularly.

2. Practice self-compassion: Treat yourself with kindness, understanding, and patience, especially when facing challenges or setbacks related to ADHD. Acknowledge that living with ADHD can be difficult, but remember that these challenges do not define your worth as a person.

3. Set realistic expectations: Adjust your expectations to be achievable and realistic, taking into account your ADHD-related challenges. Focus on progress rather than perfection, and celebrate your accomplishments, no matter how small.

4. Surround yourself with positivity: Surround yourself with supportive and understanding friends, family members, and colleagues who appreciate your unique qualities and can provide encouragement and reassurance. Avoid negative influences and seek out positive role models or mentors who inspire you.

5. Engage in activities that boost self-esteem: Participate in hobbies, interests, or activities that make you feel good about yourself and align with your strengths. Engaging in activities that you enjoy and excel at can help reinforce a positive self-image.

6. Use positive affirmations: Incorporate positive affirmations into your daily routine to remind yourself of your worth and value. Repeat affirmations that resonate with you, such as "I am capable," "I am worthy," or "I am enough." You can also create personalized affirmations based on your strengths and achievements.

7. Challenge negative self-talk: When negative thoughts about yourself arise, challenge them by asking yourself if they are based on facts or assumptions. Replace negative self-talk with more balanced, positive statements that acknowledge your strengths and accomplishments.

8. Reflect on your values: Identify the values that are most important to you, such as honesty, kindness, or perseverance. Consider how your actions align with these values and how they contribute to your self-image. Emphasizing your values can help create a more positive and authentic self-image.

In conclusion, building a positive self-image is an essential aspect of living well with ADHD. By focusing on your strengths, practicing self-compassion, setting realistic expectations, and surrounding yourself with positivity, you can foster a healthy and supportive relationship with yourself that enables you to successfully navigate the challenges of ADHD and thrive in your personal and professional life.

2.5. Overcoming Negative Self-Talk

Negative self-talk can significantly impact your self-image, self-esteem, and overall well-being, especially for individuals with ADHD. Overcoming negative self-talk involves becoming aware of these thoughts, challenging their validity, and replacing them with more balanced, positive statements. In this section, we will discuss strategies for overcoming negative self-talk when living with ADHD.

1. Develop mindfulness: Mindfulness involves paying attention to your thoughts and feelings without judgment. Practice mindfulness by observing your negative self-talk as it arises, recognizing it, and allowing it to pass without engaging with it. This can help you develop greater awareness of your thought patterns and create space for more positive self-talk.

2. Identify cognitive distortions: Cognitive distortions are irrational or exaggerated thought patterns that can contribute to negative self-talk. Common cognitive distortions include all-or-nothing thinking, overgeneralization, and catastrophizing. Recognize these distortions in your thoughts and challenge their validity.

3. Challenge negative thoughts: When negative thoughts arise, examine them critically and ask yourself whether they are based on facts or assumptions. Consider alternative explanations and perspectives, and remind yourself of your strengths and accomplishments that contradict these thoughts.

4. Replace negative thoughts with positive statements: After challenging negative thoughts, replace them with

more balanced, positive statements that acknowledge your strengths, talents, and achievements. Focus on growth and improvement, rather than perfection.

5. Practice self-compassion: Be kind, understanding, and patient with yourself, especially when facing challenges or setbacks related to ADHD. Remind yourself that it's okay to make mistakes and that everyone has strengths and weaknesses.

6. Use positive affirmations: Incorporate positive affirmations into your daily routine to counteract negative self-talk. Choose affirmations that resonate with you and reinforce your self-worth and capabilities, such as "I am strong," "I am capable," or "I am deserving of happiness."

7. Surround yourself with positivity: Seek out supportive and understanding friends, family members, or colleagues who can provide encouragement and reassurance when negative self-talk arises. Sharing your thoughts and feelings with others can help you gain new perspectives and challenge negative beliefs about yourself.

8. Seek professional help: If negative self-talk becomes overwhelming or significantly impacts your well-being, consider seeking help from a mental health professional, such as a therapist or counselor. They can provide guidance and support in identifying and overcoming negative thought patterns and building a more positive self-image.

In conclusion, overcoming negative self-talk is an essential aspect of living well with ADHD. By developing mindfulness, challenging negative thoughts, practicing self-compassion, and surrounding yourself with positivity, you can cultivate a more balanced and positive self-image that supports your overall well-being and success in managing ADHD.

Chapter 3: Organization and Time Management

3.1. Establishing Routines

Establishing routines is crucial for individuals with ADHD, as they provide structure, consistency, and predictability, which can help manage ADHD symptoms and improve overall functioning. Routines can help reduce stress, increase productivity, and promote a sense of control and accomplishment. In this section, we will discuss strategies for establishing effective routines in your daily life.

1. Identify your priorities: Before creating a routine, determine your most important tasks and responsibilities. These priorities will serve as the foundation of your routine, ensuring that you allocate adequate time and energy to the most essential aspects of your life.

2. Break tasks into smaller steps: Breaking larger tasks into smaller, more manageable steps can make them less overwhelming and easier to incorporate into your routine. This approach can also help increase your sense of accomplishment and momentum as you complete each step.

3. Schedule consistent times: Establish consistent times for activities and tasks whenever possible. For example, designate a specific time each day for exercise, meal planning, or household chores. Consistency helps reinforce routines and makes them easier to maintain.

4. Create daily, weekly, and monthly routines: Develop routines for different timeframes to address various tasks and responsibilities. Daily routines might include morning and evening rituals, while weekly routines could involve meal planning, laundry, or household cleaning. Monthly routines might encompass budgeting, goal-setting, or larger projects.

5. Allow for flexibility: While routines provide structure and predictability, it's essential to allow for some flexibility. Unexpected events or changes in your schedule may require adjustments to your routine. Be open to modifying your routine as needed, and avoid becoming overly rigid or inflexible.

6. Use visual aids: Visual aids, such as calendars, planners, or to-do lists, can help you keep track of your routines and stay organized. Choose a system that works best for you, whether it's a physical planner, a digital calendar, or a combination of both.

7. Establish routines for transitions: Develop routines for times of transition, such as waking up, going to bed, or switching between tasks. These routines can help you mentally and physically prepare for changes and maintain a sense of control and organization throughout your day.

8. Involve others: If you live with others, involve them in your routines to promote consistency and support. Sharing routines with family members or roommates can help reinforce your routines and create a more structured and supportive environment.

9. Regularly review and adjust: Periodically assess the

effectiveness of your routines and make adjustments as needed. As your priorities, responsibilities, or circumstances change, your routines may need to be updated to reflect these changes.

In conclusion, establishing routines is a vital aspect of managing ADHD effectively. By identifying your priorities, breaking tasks into smaller steps, allowing for flexibility, and using visual aids, you can create consistent and adaptable routines that promote organization, time management, and overall well-being.

3.2. Time Management Techniques

Effective time management is essential for individuals with ADHD, as it can help mitigate challenges related to focus, organization, and procrastination. By implementing various time management techniques, you can improve your productivity, reduce stress, and enhance your overall quality of life. In this section, we will discuss several time management techniques that can be beneficial for individuals with ADHD.

1. Prioritize tasks: Begin by identifying your most important tasks and prioritizing them according to their urgency, importance, and deadlines. This can help you allocate your time and energy more efficiently and ensure that critical tasks are completed in a timely manner.

2. Use a planner or calendar: Utilize a planner or calendar, whether physical or digital, to keep track of your appointments, deadlines, and responsibilities. Regularly update your planner and review it daily to stay organized and aware of upcoming tasks and events.

3. Break tasks into smaller steps: Divide larger tasks into smaller, more manageable steps, and assign deadlines for each step. This can help make tasks less overwhelming and increase your sense of accomplishment as you complete each step.

4. Set realistic goals: Establish realistic goals for yourself, taking into account your ADHD-related challenges. Avoid setting overly ambitious goals that may lead to frustration and disappointment. Instead, focus on achievable goals that align with your strengths and capabilities.

5. Utilize timers and alarms: Use timers, alarms, or apps to set time limits for tasks or to remind yourself of upcoming deadlines or appointments. These tools can help you maintain focus, avoid procrastination, and ensure that you allocate adequate time for each task.

6. Implement the Pomodoro Technique: The Pomodoro Technique involves working in short, focused intervals (typically 25 minutes) followed by a short break (usually 5 minutes). This method can help improve focus and productivity while providing regular opportunities for rest and rejuvenation.

7. Schedule regular breaks: Incorporate breaks into your daily schedule to avoid burnout and maintain focus. Use breaks to engage in relaxing activities, such as stretching, deep breathing, or taking a short walk.

8. Eliminate distractions: Identify and minimize distractions in your environment, such as noise, clutter, or electronic devices. Creating a focused and organized workspace can help improve your productivity and time management.

9. Delegate tasks: When possible, delegate tasks to others, especially if they are time-consuming or not aligned with your strengths. Delegating can help you focus on more important or enjoyable tasks while reducing your overall workload.

10. Reflect on your progress: Regularly review your time management strategies and evaluate their effectiveness. Identify areas for improvement and adjust your techniques as needed to enhance your productivity and

overall time management.

In conclusion, implementing effective time management techniques is crucial for individuals with ADHD. By prioritizing tasks, using a planner, breaking tasks into smaller steps, and employing tools such as timers and the Pomodoro Technique, you can improve your focus, organization, and productivity, leading to a more fulfilling and balanced life.

3.3. Organizational Tools and Strategies

Maintaining organization can be challenging for individuals with ADHD, but implementing various tools and strategies can help manage ADHD symptoms and improve daily functioning. By using organizational tools and strategies, you can enhance your productivity, reduce stress, and create a more structured and supportive environment. In this section, we will discuss several organizational tools and strategies that can be beneficial for individuals with ADHD.

1. Planners and calendars: Utilize planners and calendars, either physical or digital, to keep track of appointments, deadlines, and tasks. Regularly update and review your planner or calendar to stay organized and aware of your responsibilities.

2. To-do lists: Create daily, weekly, or monthly to-do lists to help you prioritize tasks and stay focused on your goals. Break larger tasks into smaller, manageable steps, and check off completed items to track your progress and boost your sense of accomplishment.

3. Color-coding: Use color-coding systems to categorize and organize various aspects of your life, such as work, personal, or family-related tasks. This visual approach can help you quickly and easily identify priorities and deadlines.

4. Labeling and categorizing: Label and categorize your belongings, documents, and files, either physically or digitally, to streamline organization and make items easier to locate. This can save time and reduce the stress associated with searching for misplaced items.

5. Declutter and simplify: Regularly declutter and simplify your living and working spaces. A clutter-free environment can help improve focus, reduce stress, and enhance overall organization.

6. Establish designated spaces: Assign designated spaces for specific items or activities, such as a dedicated workspace, a charging station for electronic devices, or a specific place for keys and other essentials. This can help maintain organization and streamline your daily routine.

7. Use storage solutions: Implement storage solutions, such as shelves, bins, or filing systems, to keep your belongings organized and easily accessible. Choose storage solutions that work best for your needs and preferences, whether they are open or closed, visible or hidden.

8. Set reminders: Use electronic reminders, sticky notes, or other visual cues to help you remember important tasks, deadlines, or appointments. Place reminders in prominent locations to ensure that you see them regularly.

9. Develop routines: As discussed in a previous section, establishing routines can help provide structure, consistency, and predictability, which are essential for managing ADHD symptoms and maintaining organization.

10. Seek support: Enlist the help of friends, family members, or professional organizers to assist you in implementing and maintaining organizational strategies. Sharing your goals and progress with others can help

provide accountability and motivation.

In conclusion, using organizational tools and strategies is crucial for individuals with ADHD. By implementing planners, to-do lists, color-coding systems, and storage solutions, you can create an organized and supportive environment that enhances your productivity, reduces stress, and improves your overall quality of life.

3.4. Prioritizing Tasks

Effectively prioritizing tasks is essential for individuals with ADHD, as it can help manage time and resources more efficiently, reduce stress, and increase productivity. By prioritizing tasks, you can ensure that your most important and time-sensitive responsibilities are addressed first. In this section, we will discuss strategies for prioritizing tasks to achieve better time management and organization.

1. Identify your goals and values: Determine your short-term and long-term goals and identify the values that guide your decisions. Your goals and values will serve as a foundation for prioritizing tasks and allocating your time and energy.

2. Assess urgency and importance: Evaluate each task based on its urgency and importance. Urgent tasks require immediate attention, while important tasks contribute to your long-term goals and values. Focus on tasks that are both urgent and important first.

3. Use the Eisenhower Matrix: The Eisenhower Matrix is a prioritization tool that categorizes tasks into four quadrants based on their urgency and importance. The quadrants are: urgent and important, important but not urgent, urgent but not important, and neither urgent nor important. Complete tasks in each quadrant according to their priority level.

4. Set deadlines: Assign deadlines to each task to create a sense of urgency and establish clear timeframes for completion. Deadlines can help prevent procrastination and ensure that tasks are completed in a timely manner.

5. Break tasks into smaller steps: Divide larger tasks into smaller, more manageable steps, and prioritize each step according to its urgency and importance. This can help make tasks less overwhelming and improve your overall organization and time management.

6. Delegate when possible: If a task can be delegated to someone else, consider doing so. Delegating tasks can free up your time and energy for more important or enjoyable activities and help you maintain focus on your priorities.

7. Reevaluate priorities regularly: Regularly assess and adjust your priorities as needed. As your goals, values, or circumstances change, your priorities may need to be updated to reflect these changes.

8. Limit the number of tasks: Avoid overloading your to-do list with too many tasks. Focus on a manageable number of tasks each day, and reevaluate your priorities if you consistently find yourself unable to complete your to-do list.

9. Use a prioritization system: Develop a system for prioritizing tasks that works best for you, whether it's a color-coding system, numbering system, or another method. Consistently using a prioritization system can help you maintain focus on your most important tasks.

10. Avoid multitasking: Focus on one task at a time rather than attempting to multitask. Multitasking can decrease productivity and make it more challenging to prioritize and complete tasks efficiently.

In conclusion, effectively prioritizing tasks is a critical aspect of managing ADHD. By identifying your goals and values, assessing the urgency and importance of tasks, using tools like the Eisenhower Matrix, and breaking tasks into smaller steps, you can improve your time management, organization, and overall productivity, leading to a more fulfilling and balanced life.

3.5. Breaking Tasks into Manageable Steps

Breaking tasks into smaller, more manageable steps is a highly effective strategy for individuals with ADHD, as it can help combat feelings of overwhelm, improve focus, and increase the likelihood of task completion. By dividing tasks into manageable steps, you can create a clear roadmap for success and boost your overall productivity. In this section, we will discuss strategies for breaking tasks into manageable steps.

1. Analyze the task: Begin by analyzing the task at hand and identifying its main components. This will help you gain a better understanding of the task's scope and complexity, and will enable you to break it down into smaller steps more effectively.

2. Create a step-by-step plan: List each step required to complete the task in a logical and sequential order. This plan will serve as a guide to help you navigate through the task and keep you focused on the steps necessary for completion.

3. Assign deadlines: Assign a deadline for each step of the task. Deadlines create a sense of urgency and help ensure that you make consistent progress toward completing the task.

4. Prioritize steps: Prioritize the steps based on their importance, urgency, or dependencies on other steps. This will help you determine which steps to tackle first and help you allocate your time and energy more efficiently.

5. Keep steps specific and achievable: Ensure that each step is specific, actionable, and achievable within a reasonable timeframe. This will help you avoid becoming overwhelmed and increase your sense of accomplishment as you complete each step.

6. Use visual aids: Utilize visual aids, such as checklists, flowcharts, or mind maps, to help you visualize the steps and track your progress. Visual aids can also serve as a reminder of the steps you need to complete and help you stay organized.

7. Break down larger steps: If a step still feels overwhelming or complex, break it down into smaller sub-steps. This can make the task even more manageable and help you maintain your momentum as you work through each step.

8. Monitor your progress: Regularly review your progress and adjust your plan as needed. If you encounter obstacles or challenges, reevaluate your approach and modify the steps accordingly.

9. Celebrate milestones: Acknowledge and celebrate your progress as you complete each step. Rewarding yourself for your achievements can help boost your motivation and maintain your momentum throughout the task.

10. Seek support: If you find it challenging to break tasks into manageable steps, consider seeking support from friends, family, or a coach. They can provide valuable insights, encouragement, and accountability to help you succeed.

In conclusion, breaking tasks into manageable steps is a powerful strategy for managing ADHD and improving productivity. By analyzing the task, creating a step-by-step plan, assigning deadlines, and using visual aids, you can tackle tasks more effectively and maintain your focus and motivation throughout the process.

4.1. Understanding the ADHD Brain and Focus

The challenges associated with focus and concentration are common among individuals with ADHD. To effectively improve focus and concentration, it's important to first understand how the ADHD brain functions in relation to these aspects. In this section, we will delve into the neuroscience behind the ADHD brain and its impact on focus and concentration.

1. Neurotransmitters and ADHD: Neurotransmitters, such as dopamine and norepinephrine, play a crucial role in attention and focus. Research suggests that individuals with ADHD may have imbalances or dysregulation in these neurotransmitters, leading to difficulties with focus and concentration.

2. Executive functioning: Executive functions are a set of cognitive processes that involve the prefrontal cortex of the brain. These processes include working memory, cognitive flexibility, and inhibitory control. People with ADHD often experience challenges with executive functioning, which can contribute to difficulties with focus and concentration.

3. Hyperfocus: Interestingly, individuals with ADHD may also experience hyperfocus, a state of intense concentration on a single task or activity to the exclusion of other stimuli. While this can be beneficial in certain situations, it can also lead to an imbalance in attention distribution and difficulty disengaging from the task at hand.

4. Sensory processing: People with ADHD may also have heightened sensitivity to external stimuli, making

it challenging to filter out irrelevant information and focus on the task at hand. This sensitivity can contribute to distractions and difficulties in maintaining concentration.

5. Emotional regulation: Emotional regulation is another aspect of executive functioning that can be affected by ADHD. Challenges with emotional regulation can lead to increased frustration, stress, or anxiety, which can further exacerbate difficulties with focus and concentration.

Now that we have explored the factors that contribute to focus and concentration challenges in individuals with ADHD, we can better understand the need for tailored strategies to address these issues. In the following sections, we will discuss various approaches, techniques, and tools to help improve focus and concentration, taking into consideration the unique aspects of the ADHD brain.

4.2. Mindfulness and Meditation Practices

Mindfulness and meditation practices can be particularly beneficial for individuals with ADHD, as they promote awareness, focus, and self-regulation. These practices can help train the mind to be more present, reduce stress, and improve overall well-being. In this section, we will explore various mindfulness and meditation practices that can be incorporated into daily life to enhance focus and concentration.

1. Mindful breathing: Mindful breathing involves focusing your attention on your breath as it flows in and out of your body. This practice can help anchor your thoughts and bring your awareness back to the present moment, making it easier to maintain focus.

2. Body scan meditation: Body scan meditation involves systematically directing your attention to different parts of your body, noticing any sensations or tension. This practice encourages a deeper connection between the mind and body and can help you become more aware of distractions or discomfort that may be affecting your focus.

3. Guided meditation: Guided meditation involves following a recorded meditation led by an experienced practitioner. These meditations can be tailored to specific needs, such as improving focus, reducing stress, or promoting relaxation, and are particularly helpful for beginners.

4. Loving-kindness meditation: Loving-kindness meditation, or metta meditation, involves cultivating feelings of compassion and love for oneself and others.

This practice can help improve emotional regulation, reduce negative self-talk, and enhance overall well-being, contributing to better focus and concentration.

5. Mindfulness-based stress reduction (MBSR): MBSR is a structured program that combines mindfulness meditation, body awareness, and yoga to promote stress reduction and improve focus. The program has been widely studied and has demonstrated positive effects on mental health and well-being.

6. Walking meditation: Walking meditation involves focusing on the sensations of your body and breath while walking slowly and deliberately. This practice combines mindfulness with gentle physical activity, providing an alternative for those who struggle with seated meditation.

7. Yoga: Yoga incorporates mindfulness, breathwork, and physical movement, helping to improve focus, reduce stress, and promote overall well-being. Regular yoga practice can help individuals with ADHD cultivate greater self-awareness and improve their ability to concentrate.

Incorporating mindfulness and meditation practices into your daily routine can have a significant impact on your ability to focus and concentrate. By exploring different techniques, you can discover the approaches that resonate best with you and help you achieve greater focus, self-regulation, and emotional balance.

4.3. Creating a Conducive Work Environment

A conducive work environment can significantly improve focus and concentration, especially for individuals with ADHD who may be more sensitive to external stimuli. By optimizing your workspace and surroundings, you can minimize distractions, enhance productivity, and support overall well-being. In this section, we will discuss various strategies for creating a conducive work environment.

1. Declutter your space: Keep your workspace clean and organized to minimize distractions and make it easier to find what you need. A clutter-free environment can help promote mental clarity and improve focus.

2. Limit noise distractions: Use noise-cancelling headphones, white noise machines, or calming background music to reduce auditory distractions. Alternatively, choose a quiet space to work in, away from noisy environments or high-traffic areas.

3. Optimize lighting: Ensure your workspace has adequate lighting, preferably natural light, to reduce eye strain and improve alertness. If natural light is limited, use adjustable lamps or consider investing in light therapy devices to simulate daylight.

4. Personalize your space: Personalize your workspace with items that inspire, motivate, or bring you joy, such as photographs, artwork, or motivational quotes. A positive and personalized work environment can help boost mood and improve focus.

5. Ergonomics: Invest in ergonomic furniture and

accessories, such as adjustable chairs, standing desks, or keyboard trays, to promote comfort and reduce the risk of strain or injury. A comfortable workspace can help improve concentration and productivity.

6. Set boundaries: Establish clear boundaries between your workspace and personal space, particularly if you work from home. This separation can help create a mental shift between work and relaxation, making it easier to focus during work hours.

7. Minimize digital distractions: Limit digital distractions by closing unnecessary browser tabs, turning off notifications, or using website blockers to restrict access to distracting sites. Establish designated times for checking email and social media to avoid constant interruptions.

8. Incorporate plants: Adding greenery to your workspace can improve air quality, reduce stress, and boost mood. Studies have shown that plants can enhance productivity and cognitive performance.

9. Organize materials: Use organizational tools like shelves, file cabinets, or desk organizers to keep your materials and supplies easily accessible and orderly. This can help prevent wasted time searching for items and maintain a more focused mindset.

10. Establish a routine: Create a consistent daily routine that includes breaks and periods of focused work. This structure can help regulate your energy levels and improve your ability to concentrate on tasks.

By implementing these strategies, you can create a work environment that supports focus, concentration, and productivity. A conducive workspace, tailored to your specific needs and preferences, can help you effectively manage ADHD symptoms and enhance overall well-being.

4.4. Minimizing Distractions

Minimizing distractions is essential for individuals with ADHD, as they may have a heightened sensitivity to external stimuli and a reduced ability to filter out irrelevant information. By proactively managing potential distractions, you can improve focus, concentration, and overall productivity. In this section, we will discuss various strategies for minimizing distractions in your daily life.

1. Identify your distractions: Begin by identifying the distractions that most commonly disrupt your focus. These might include social media, email, noise, or specific tasks that tend to pull your attention away from your primary goals.

2. Prioritize tasks: Prioritize your tasks and allocate dedicated time for each. By having a clear plan for your day, you can reduce the likelihood of getting sidetracked by less important tasks or distractions.

3. Schedule breaks: Regularly scheduled breaks can help prevent burnout and maintain focus throughout the day. Use these breaks to address potential distractions, such as checking email or social media, so they don't interfere with your focused work periods.

4. Use technology wisely: Utilize productivity apps, website blockers, or focus-enhancing tools to minimize digital distractions. Adjust notification settings on your devices to reduce interruptions and create a more focused digital environment.

5. Set boundaries: Communicate your need for focused work time to family members, roommates, or coworkers. Establish clear boundaries and expectations to minimize interruptions and maintain concentration.

6. Designate a distraction-free zone: Create a dedicated workspace or area in your home that is free from distractions. This space should be reserved exclusively for focused work or study, helping to create a mental association between the environment and concentration.

7. Practice mindfulness: Incorporate mindfulness techniques, such as deep breathing or meditation, to help you become more aware of your thoughts and distractions. By increasing your awareness, you can more effectively redirect your focus when distractions arise.

8. Use timers: Use tools like the Pomodoro Technique or other time management methods to break your work into focused intervals, followed by short breaks. This approach can help maintain your concentration and prevent distractions from derailing your progress.

9. Remove physical distractions: Keep your workspace clutter-free and organized, removing any items or objects that may distract you. Ensure that necessary materials and tools are easily accessible to minimize disruptions during focused work periods.

10. Reflect and adjust: Regularly assess your progress in minimizing distractions and identify areas for improvement. By reflecting on your experiences, you can develop a better understanding of your specific needs and make adjustments to further enhance your focus and

concentration.

By implementing these strategies, you can effectively minimize distractions and create an environment that supports focus, concentration, and productivity. Managing distractions is an ongoing process, and it's essential to remain adaptable and open to change as your needs and circumstances evolve.

4.5. Techniques to Improve Concentration

Improving concentration is crucial for individuals with ADHD to enhance productivity and overall well-being. By incorporating various techniques and strategies into your daily routine, you can train your mind to better focus on tasks and maintain concentration. In this section, we will discuss several techniques to help improve concentration.

1. Practice single-tasking: Focus on one task at a time, rather than attempting to multitask. Single-tasking allows you to direct your full attention to the task at hand, increasing the likelihood of completing it efficiently and effectively.

2. Utilize focus-enhancing tools: Explore tools and apps designed to improve concentration, such as focus timers, noise-cancelling headphones, or brain training exercises. These tools can help create an environment that supports focus and concentration.

3. Establish daily routines: Create consistent daily routines for work, meals, exercise, and sleep. These routines can help regulate your energy levels, reduce stress, and enhance your ability to concentrate on tasks.

4. Take regular breaks: Schedule short breaks throughout your day to recharge and prevent burnout. Use techniques like the Pomodoro Technique to balance focused work periods with restorative breaks.

5. Exercise regularly: Engage in regular physical activity to improve mental clarity, increase energy levels, and reduce stress. Exercise has been shown to enhance

cognitive function and support focus and concentration.

6. Prioritize sleep: Prioritize getting enough quality sleep, as sleep deprivation can significantly impact concentration and cognitive function. Establish healthy sleep habits and create a sleep-friendly environment to promote restorative rest.

7. Manage stress: Practice stress management techniques, such as deep breathing, meditation, or progressive muscle relaxation, to reduce the impact of stress on focus and concentration.

8. Stay hydrated and eat well: Ensure you are adequately hydrated and maintain a balanced diet. Proper nutrition and hydration can positively influence brain function and support focus and concentration.

9. Break tasks into smaller steps: Divide complex tasks into smaller, manageable steps to reduce feelings of overwhelm and improve focus. Tackle one step at a time, celebrating progress along the way.

10. Set specific goals: Establish clear and specific goals for your tasks, and keep these goals in mind as you work. This can help you maintain focus on the desired outcome and increase motivation to complete the task.

By incorporating these techniques into your daily life, you can gradually improve your concentration and better manage ADHD symptoms. Remember that change takes time, and it's essential to be patient and persistent in your efforts to enhance focus and concentration. Regularly assess your progress and adjust your strategies as needed to support your unique needs and circumstances.

Chapter 5: Emotional Regulation

5.1. Identifying and Managing Emotions

Emotional regulation is a critical skill for individuals with ADHD, as they may experience heightened emotions or difficulty controlling emotional responses. Learning to identify and manage emotions can improve relationships, communication, and overall well-being. In this section, we will explore various strategies for identifying and managing emotions effectively.

1. Emotional awareness: Begin by cultivating emotional awareness, recognizing and acknowledging the emotions you experience throughout the day. This can help you become more attuned to your emotional state and identify patterns or triggers that may impact your emotional well-being.

2. Practice mindfulness: Engage in mindfulness practices, such as meditation or deep breathing exercises, to help you observe your emotions without judgment. This can promote greater self-awareness and self-acceptance, making it easier to manage emotions effectively.

3. Keep a mood journal: Track your emotions and their triggers in a mood journal. This can help you identify patterns and better understand the factors that contribute to your emotional state.

4. Develop a healthy emotional vocabulary: Expand your emotional vocabulary to more accurately express and understand your feelings. By naming your emotions, you can gain greater control over them and communicate

more effectively with others.

5. Engage in self-reflection: Regularly assess your emotional experiences and consider the factors that may be influencing your emotions. Reflect on your reactions to situations and explore alternative responses that may be more adaptive or constructive.

6. Implement self-soothing techniques: Develop a toolkit of self-soothing strategies, such as deep breathing exercises, progressive muscle relaxation, or visualization, to help you calm down during periods of heightened emotion.

7. Seek social support: Connect with friends, family members, or support groups to discuss your emotions and experiences. Sharing your feelings with others can help reduce feelings of isolation and provide valuable insight and guidance.

8. Practice self-compassion: Treat yourself with kindness and understanding when you experience difficult emotions. Acknowledge that it's normal to feel a range of emotions, and avoid self-criticism or judgment.

9. Set boundaries: Establish and maintain healthy boundaries in your relationships to protect your emotional well-being. Communicate your needs and limits clearly, and respect the boundaries of others.

10. Seek professional help: If you continue to struggle with emotional regulation, consider seeking the support of a mental health professional, such as a therapist or counselor. They can help you develop personalized

strategies to manage your emotions more effectively.

By implementing these strategies, you can enhance your emotional regulation skills and improve your ability to manage the challenges associated with ADHD. Remember that emotional regulation is an ongoing process, and it's essential to be patient and persistent in your efforts to develop and maintain these skills.

5.2. Coping Mechanisms for Stress and Anxiety

Stress and anxiety are common challenges for individuals with ADHD, and learning effective coping mechanisms is essential for maintaining emotional well-being. In this section, we will discuss various strategies for managing stress and anxiety, which can ultimately improve your emotional regulation skills.

1. Practice mindfulness: Incorporate mindfulness techniques, such as meditation, deep breathing exercises, or progressive muscle relaxation, into your daily routine. These practices can help reduce stress, increase self-awareness, and promote emotional regulation.

2. Develop a self-care routine: Prioritize self-care activities that help you relax and recharge, such as engaging in hobbies, spending time in nature, or practicing yoga. Regular self-care can help build resilience to stress and anxiety.

3. Establish a support network: Build a network of supportive friends, family members, or peers who understand your challenges and can offer guidance and encouragement. Having a strong support system can help you better cope with stress and anxiety.

4. Get regular exercise: Participate in regular physical activity to reduce stress, boost mood, and improve overall well-being. Exercise has been shown to have numerous mental health benefits, including reduced symptoms of anxiety and depression.

5. Prioritize sleep: Ensure you get enough quality

sleep, as poor sleep can exacerbate stress and anxiety. Develop healthy sleep habits and create a sleep-friendly environment to promote restorative rest.

6. Maintain a balanced diet: Eat a well-balanced diet rich in whole foods, lean protein, and healthy fats to support overall health and well-being. Proper nutrition can help regulate mood and reduce anxiety.

7. Break tasks into smaller steps: Break complex tasks into smaller, manageable steps to reduce feelings of overwhelm and stress. Tackle one step at a time, and celebrate your progress along the way.

8. Set realistic goals: Establish achievable and realistic goals for yourself to avoid undue stress and anxiety. Recognize that perfection is unattainable, and focus on progress rather than perfection.

9. Practice time management: Develop effective time management strategies to help you stay organized and reduce stress. Create daily schedules, prioritize tasks, and allocate dedicated time for work, leisure, and self-care.

10. Seek professional help: If stress and anxiety continue to be overwhelming, consider seeking the support of a mental health professional, such as a therapist or counselor. They can help you develop personalized strategies to cope with stress and anxiety more effectively.

By implementing these coping mechanisms, you can better manage stress and anxiety, improving your emotional regulation and overall well-being. Remember that managing stress and anxiety is an ongoing process, and it's essential to be patient and persistent in your efforts to develop and maintain these skills.

5.3. Developing Emotional Resilience

Emotional resilience refers to the ability to adapt and cope with challenging situations, stressors, or setbacks. For individuals with ADHD, developing emotional resilience is crucial for maintaining emotional well-being and successfully navigating life's challenges. In this section, we will explore various strategies to cultivate emotional resilience.

1. Foster a growth mindset: Embrace challenges and view setbacks as opportunities for learning and growth. Cultivate a growth mindset by focusing on personal development and recognizing that abilities can be developed through dedication and effort.

2. Practice self-compassion: Treat yourself with kindness and understanding when facing difficult situations or emotions. Acknowledge that everyone experiences setbacks and challenges, and avoid self-criticism or judgment during these times.

3. Cultivate optimism: Maintain a positive outlook and focus on the aspects of a situation that are within your control. Practice gratitude by acknowledging the good things in your life and the progress you've made.

4. Develop problem-solving skills: Improve your ability to identify and address problems by breaking them down into smaller, manageable steps. Approach problems with curiosity and creativity, seeking out new solutions and perspectives.

5. Establish a support network: Build a network of

supportive friends, family members, or peers who understand your challenges and can offer guidance and encouragement. Having a strong support system can help you better cope with setbacks and build resilience.

6. Set realistic goals: Establish achievable and realistic goals for yourself, and regularly reassess and adjust them as needed. This can help maintain motivation and prevent feelings of overwhelm or frustration.

7. Engage in self-reflection: Regularly assess your experiences, emotions, and reactions to situations. Reflect on your growth and progress, and use this insight to guide your future actions and decisions.

8. Prioritize self-care: Ensure that your physical, emotional, and mental well-being are cared for through regular self-care activities, such as exercise, sleep, and hobbies. Taking care of yourself can provide a strong foundation for building emotional resilience.

9. Embrace adaptability: Be open to change and recognize that setbacks and challenges are a natural part of life. Develop the ability to adapt and adjust to new circumstances, and be willing to reevaluate your goals and plans as needed.

10. Seek professional help: If you continue to struggle with developing emotional resilience, consider seeking the support of a mental health professional, such as a therapist or counselor. They can help you develop personalized strategies to cultivate resilience and manage your emotions more effectively.

By implementing these strategies, you can develop emotional resilience, which will support your emotional well-being and help you navigate the challenges associated with ADHD. Remember that building emotional resilience takes time and consistent effort, so be patient and persistent in your journey toward greater emotional strength.

5.4. Mind-Body Connection and Self-Care

The mind-body connection plays a significant role in emotional well-being, particularly for individuals with ADHD. Engaging in regular self-care activities that support both mental and physical health can have a positive impact on emotional regulation. In this section, we will discuss the importance of the mind-body connection and explore various self-care practices to enhance overall well-being.

1. Exercise regularly: Participate in regular physical activity to improve mood, reduce stress, and support cognitive function. Exercise has been shown to have numerous mental health benefits, including increased focus and concentration, which are essential for individuals with ADHD.

2. Maintain a balanced diet: Prioritize a well-balanced diet rich in whole foods, lean protein, and healthy fats. Proper nutrition supports brain function, mood regulation, and overall health, contributing to a stronger mind-body connection.

3. Prioritize sleep: Ensure you get enough quality sleep, as sleep deprivation can negatively impact both physical and emotional well-being. Develop healthy sleep habits and create a sleep-friendly environment to promote restorative rest.

4. Practice mindfulness: Engage in mindfulness practices, such as meditation, deep breathing exercises, or yoga, to promote relaxation and enhance the mind-body connection. These practices can help improve self-awareness, emotional regulation, and stress management.

5. Engage in hobbies: Participate in activities that bring joy and relaxation, such as reading, painting, or gardening. Hobbies can help reduce stress, improve mood, and foster a sense of accomplishment.

6. Connect with nature: Spend time outdoors in natural settings to reduce stress, improve mood, and boost overall well-being. Nature has been shown to have numerous mental health benefits, including increased feelings of happiness and reduced symptoms of anxiety and depression.

7. Build social connections: Foster strong relationships with friends, family members, or peers who can provide emotional support and understanding. Social connections are essential for emotional well-being and can help buffer against stress and adversity.

8. Develop relaxation techniques: Learn and practice relaxation techniques, such as progressive muscle relaxation, guided imagery, or deep breathing exercises, to manage stress and promote a stronger mind-body connection.

9. Set boundaries: Establish and maintain healthy boundaries in your personal and professional life to protect your emotional and physical well-being. Communicate your needs and limits clearly and respect the boundaries of others.

10. Seek professional help: If needed, consult with mental health professionals or healthcare providers to address any concerns related to your emotional or physical well-being. They can help you develop personalized strategies

to support your mind-body connection and overall well-being.

By prioritizing self-care activities that nurture both your mind and body, you can strengthen the mind-body connection and support your emotional regulation. Remember that self-care is an ongoing process, and it's essential to be patient and persistent in your efforts to maintain a healthy mind-body balance.

5.5. Seeking Professional Help

There may be times when individuals with ADHD need additional support to effectively manage their emotions and navigate challenges in their lives. Seeking professional help can provide valuable guidance, personalized strategies, and coping mechanisms. In this section, we will discuss the benefits of seeking professional help and the types of professionals you can consult for support.

1. Psychotherapy: Psychotherapy, such as cognitive-behavioral therapy (CBT) or dialectical behavior therapy (DBT), can help individuals with ADHD develop effective strategies for emotional regulation, stress management, and coping with challenges. Therapists can provide a safe, non-judgmental space to explore emotions, thoughts, and behaviors, and help identify and address patterns that may be contributing to difficulties.

2. Counseling: Counselors can offer guidance and support to help individuals navigate life's challenges and improve their emotional well-being. Counseling can provide a safe environment to discuss feelings, concerns, and experiences, while receiving valuable feedback and coping strategies.

3. Psychiatric care: Psychiatrists or psychiatric nurse practitioners can evaluate and diagnose ADHD, as well as prescribe and monitor medications, if necessary. Medication can be an essential component of managing ADHD symptoms and improving emotional regulation for some individuals.

4. Coaching: ADHD coaches specialize in working with

individuals with ADHD to develop personalized strategies for managing their symptoms, including emotional regulation. Coaches can provide practical tips and techniques to help clients build skills, set goals, and maintain progress.

5. Support groups: Joining a support group for individuals with ADHD can provide an opportunity to connect with others who share similar experiences and challenges. Support groups can offer a sense of belonging, validation, and camaraderie, as well as practical advice and coping strategies.

6. Family therapy: Family therapy can help families affected by ADHD learn to communicate more effectively, resolve conflicts, and support one another. Family therapists can provide strategies for managing ADHD-related challenges and fostering a more harmonious family environment.

7. Educational resources: School psychologists or special education teachers can provide guidance and resources for managing ADHD symptoms in the educational setting. They can help implement accommodations, develop learning strategies, and provide emotional support for students with ADHD.

8. Occupational therapy: Occupational therapists can help individuals with ADHD develop strategies for managing daily tasks, improving organizational skills, and enhancing emotional regulation. They may also provide support for adapting to work or school environments.

When seeking professional help, it's essential to find a provider who is knowledgeable about ADHD and has experience working with individuals who have the condition. Research potential providers, ask for recommendations, and schedule an initial consultation to ensure you feel comfortable and confident with your choice.

By seeking professional help, individuals with ADHD can gain valuable insight, support, and resources for managing their emotions and overcoming challenges. Remember that seeking help is a sign of strength, not weakness, and can significantly improve your emotional well-being and overall quality of life.

Chapter 6: Nutrition and Exercise

6.1. The Role of Nutrition in ADHD Management

Nutrition plays a crucial role in managing ADHD symptoms and promoting overall well-being. A well-balanced diet can support brain function, stabilize mood, and improve focus, concentration, and emotional regulation. In this section, we will discuss the importance of nutrition in ADHD management and provide guidance for adopting a healthier diet.

1. Balanced macronutrients: Ensure your diet includes a balance of carbohydrates, proteins, and healthy fats. Carbohydrates provide the brain with energy, proteins supply essential amino acids for neurotransmitter production, and healthy fats support brain function and cellular health.

2. Opt for whole foods: Focus on consuming nutrient-dense, minimally processed whole foods, such as fruits, vegetables, whole grains, lean proteins, and healthy fats. These foods provide essential vitamins, minerals, and antioxidants that support brain health and overall well-being.

3. Omega-3 fatty acids: Incorporate omega-3 fatty acids, found in foods like fatty fish (salmon, mackerel, sardines), flaxseeds, and walnuts, into your diet. Omega-3s have been shown to support brain function, reduce inflammation, and improve ADHD symptoms in some individuals.

4. Maintain stable blood sugar levels: Eat regular

meals and snacks to prevent blood sugar fluctuations that can exacerbate ADHD symptoms. Opt for complex carbohydrates, such as whole grains, legumes, and starchy vegetables, which provide steady energy and help maintain focus and concentration.

5. Limit processed foods and additives: Reduce your intake of processed foods, artificial colors, and preservatives, as these can contribute to inflammation and exacerbate ADHD symptoms in some individuals. Focus on consuming whole, natural foods instead.

6. Stay hydrated: Adequate hydration is essential for optimal brain function and overall health. Aim to drink plenty of water throughout the day to support cognitive function and emotional regulation.

7. Consider vitamin and mineral supplementation: Some individuals with ADHD may benefit from vitamin and mineral supplementation, such as iron, zinc, magnesium, or B-vitamins. Consult with a healthcare professional to determine if supplementation is appropriate for you and to receive personalized recommendations.

8. Monitor caffeine and sugar intake: Limit your consumption of caffeine and added sugars, as these can contribute to ADHD symptoms, such as restlessness, irritability, and difficulty concentrating. Opt for healthier alternatives, such as herbal tea or naturally sweetened beverages.

9. Customize your diet: Recognize that individual dietary needs may vary, and be willing to experiment with different foods and nutrients to determine what works best for you. Keep a food diary to track your diet and

monitor its impact on your ADHD symptoms.

10. Consult a nutrition professional: If needed, consult with a registered dietitian or nutritionist who has experience working with individuals with ADHD. They can provide personalized guidance and support for implementing a healthier diet that supports ADHD management.

By prioritizing good nutrition, individuals with ADHD can support brain function, improve focus and concentration, and enhance overall well-being. Remember that dietary changes may take time to yield noticeable results, so be patient and persistent in your efforts to adopt a healthier, more balanced diet.

6.2. Healthy Eating Habits and Recommendations

Adopting healthy eating habits is essential for individuals with ADHD to support brain function, mood, and overall well-being. In this section, we will discuss practical recommendations for developing healthier eating habits that can help manage ADHD symptoms.

1. Plan meals and snacks: Prepare a weekly meal plan that includes a variety of whole foods, lean proteins, healthy fats, and complex carbohydrates. This can help ensure you're consuming a balanced diet that supports ADHD management.

2. Stick to a regular eating schedule: Eat meals and snacks at consistent times throughout the day to maintain stable blood sugar levels and minimize ADHD symptoms, such as irritability and difficulty concentrating.

3. Eat mindfully: Practice mindful eating by paying attention to your hunger and fullness cues, eating slowly, and savoring each bite. This can help prevent overeating and promote better digestion.

4. Control portion sizes: Be mindful of portion sizes, particularly for calorie-dense foods. Use measuring cups, spoons, or a food scale to ensure you're consuming appropriate portions.

5. Limit processed foods: Reduce your intake of processed and convenience foods, which can be high in added sugars, unhealthy fats, and artificial additives. Focus on consuming whole, natural foods instead.

6. Cook at home: Prepare meals at home as often as possible to control ingredients and portion sizes. Experiment with new recipes and cooking techniques to make healthy meals enjoyable and satisfying.

7. Read food labels: Familiarize yourself with food labels and ingredient lists to make informed choices about the products you consume. Look for items with minimal added sugars, artificial ingredients, and unhealthy fats.

8. Make healthier swaps: Replace unhealthy food choices with more nutritious alternatives. For example, opt for whole-grain bread instead of white bread, or choose fresh fruit over sugary desserts.

9. Practice moderation: Allow yourself occasional treats in moderation, without feeling guilty. This can help prevent feelings of deprivation and support a sustainable, balanced diet.

10. Seek professional guidance: If you're unsure about your nutritional needs or struggle to maintain healthy eating habits, consult with a registered dietitian or nutritionist. They can provide personalized recommendations and support to help you develop and maintain a healthier diet.

By incorporating these healthy eating habits and recommendations, individuals with ADHD can support brain function, mood, and overall well-being. Remember that adopting new habits takes time and persistence, so be patient and committed to making lasting changes for better ADHD management.

6.3. Exercise and its Impact on ADHD Symptoms

Regular physical activity has been shown to provide numerous benefits for individuals with ADHD, including improved focus, concentration, mood, and overall well-being. In this section, we will discuss the impact of exercise on ADHD symptoms and provide guidance for incorporating physical activity into your daily routine.

1. Enhanced focus and concentration: Exercise increases blood flow to the brain, providing it with essential nutrients and oxygen, which can improve cognitive function, attention, and memory. Regular physical activity has been shown to help individuals with ADHD maintain focus and concentration for extended periods.

2. Improved mood and emotional regulation: Exercise stimulates the production of endorphins, serotonin, and other neurotransmitters that support mood regulation and emotional well-being. Regular physical activity can help reduce feelings of anxiety, stress, and depression, which are often associated with ADHD.

3. Increased energy and motivation: Engaging in regular exercise can help boost energy levels and combat fatigue, which can be particularly beneficial for individuals with ADHD who may struggle with motivation and productivity.

4. Better sleep: Physical activity can improve sleep quality by regulating circadian rhythms and promoting deeper, more restorative sleep. Adequate sleep is crucial for managing ADHD symptoms and supporting overall well-being.

5. Enhanced self-esteem and confidence: Exercise can help improve body image and foster a sense of accomplishment, which can boost self-esteem and confidence in individuals with ADHD.

6. Stress reduction: Physical activity can serve as a healthy outlet for stress and tension, helping to reduce the impact of stress on ADHD symptoms and overall well-being.

7. Improved executive function: Regular exercise has been shown to support the development and function of the brain's prefrontal cortex, which is responsible for executive function skills, such as planning, organization, and impulse control.

To maximize the benefits of exercise for ADHD management, consider the following recommendations:

1. Choose enjoyable activities: Engage in physical activities that you enjoy and find motivating, such as swimming, hiking, dancing, or team sports. This can increase the likelihood that you will maintain a consistent exercise routine.

2. Set realistic goals: Establish achievable fitness goals that are specific, measurable, and time-bound. Regularly track your progress and celebrate your accomplishments to maintain motivation.

3. Create a routine: Schedule regular workout sessions and incorporate physical activity into your daily routine. Aim for at least 30 minutes of moderate-intensity

exercise most days of the week.

4. Start slow and gradually increase intensity: Begin with low-impact exercises and gradually increase intensity and duration as your fitness level improves. This can help prevent injury and promote long-term adherence to your exercise routine.

5. Seek social support: Join a fitness class, team sport, or workout group to foster accountability, motivation, and camaraderie.

6. Consult with a professional: If needed, consult with a personal trainer or healthcare provider for guidance on developing a safe and effective exercise routine tailored to your needs and abilities.

By incorporating regular exercise into your daily routine, individuals with ADHD can experience significant improvements in focus, concentration, mood, and overall well-being. Remember that consistency is key, so be patient and persistent in your efforts to maintain a regular exercise routine for optimal ADHD management.

6.4. Incorporating Regular Physical Activity

Developing a consistent exercise routine is crucial for individuals with ADHD to experience the full benefits of physical activity on symptom management. In this section, we will provide practical tips for incorporating regular physical activity into your daily life.

1. Schedule exercise sessions: Treat exercise like any other important appointment or task by scheduling it in your calendar. This will help prioritize physical activity and make it a consistent part of your daily routine.

2. Break it up: If you struggle to find time for a 30-minute workout, consider breaking it into shorter 10- or 15-minute sessions throughout the day. Shorter bursts of physical activity can still provide significant benefits and may be easier to fit into a busy schedule.

3. Make it a habit: Establish a consistent time for exercise, such as first thing in the morning, during your lunch break, or after work. Over time, regular exercise will become a habit that feels natural and enjoyable.

4. Find an exercise buddy: Partner with a friend or family member who has similar fitness goals. Having an exercise buddy can increase motivation, accountability, and enjoyment of physical activity.

5. Engage in activities you enjoy: Choose physical activities that you find enjoyable and motivating. This will make it more likely that you will stick to your exercise routine in the long term.

6. Mix it up: Incorporate a variety of activities, such as cardio, strength training, and flexibility exercises, to maintain interest and challenge your body in different ways. This can help prevent boredom and promote overall fitness.

7. Set realistic goals: Establish achievable short-term and long-term fitness goals that are specific, measurable, and time-bound. Regularly track your progress and celebrate your accomplishments to stay motivated.

8. Use technology: Take advantage of fitness apps, wearable devices, or online resources to track your progress, set reminders, and stay motivated.

9. Prioritize active transportation: Incorporate physical activity into your daily commute by walking, biking, or using public transportation. This can help increase your daily activity level and promote a more active lifestyle.

10. Seek professional guidance: If needed, consult with a personal trainer or healthcare provider for guidance on developing a safe and effective exercise routine tailored to your needs and abilities.

By following these tips, individuals with ADHD can successfully incorporate regular physical activity into their daily routine. Over time, consistent exercise can lead to significant improvements in focus, concentration, mood, and overall well-being, supporting effective ADHD management.

6.5. Balancing Diet and Exercise

Achieving a balance between diet and exercise is essential for individuals with ADHD to optimize symptom management and promote overall well-being. In this section, we will discuss practical tips for maintaining a balanced approach to both nutrition and physical activity.

1. Consistency is key: Prioritize consistency in both your diet and exercise routine. Eating a balanced diet and engaging in regular physical activity will have a greater impact on ADHD management when practiced consistently over time.

2. Monitor your energy levels: Pay attention to how your diet and exercise habits affect your energy levels, mood, and ADHD symptoms. Use this information to make adjustments as needed to optimize your well-being.

3. Fuel your body: Ensure you are consuming adequate calories and nutrients to support your exercise routine. Proper nutrition is essential for maintaining energy levels, supporting muscle recovery, and promoting overall health.

4. Pre- and post-workout nutrition: Plan your meals and snacks to provide optimal energy and support recovery. Consume a mix of carbohydrates and protein before and after your workouts to fuel your body and promote muscle repair.

5. Hydration: Maintain proper hydration by drinking plenty of water throughout the day, especially before, during, and after exercise. Adequate hydration supports

optimal brain function, exercise performance, and overall health.

6. Quality over quantity: Focus on the quality of the foods you consume and the types of exercise you engage in. Opt for nutrient-dense whole foods and a variety of physical activities that challenge your body and support your mental well-being.

7. Set realistic goals: Establish achievable short-term and long-term goals for both your diet and exercise routine. Regularly track your progress and celebrate your accomplishments to stay motivated.

8. Listen to your body: Pay attention to your body's signals and adjust your diet and exercise routine accordingly. If you're feeling overly tired, stressed, or unwell, consider modifying your workouts or seeking professional guidance.

9. Seek support: Consult with a registered dietitian, nutritionist, personal trainer, or healthcare provider for personalized guidance and support in balancing your diet and exercise routine. They can provide expert advice and help you develop a sustainable plan tailored to your unique needs and goals.

10. Enjoy the journey: Remember that balancing diet and exercise is a lifelong commitment. Focus on the process and the small improvements you make along the way, rather than solely on the end goal. This will help promote a sustainable, balanced approach to managing ADHD symptoms and supporting overall well-being.

By maintaining a balanced approach to diet and exercise, individuals with ADHD can experience significant improvements in focus, concentration, mood, and overall well-being. Remember that consistency and patience are key to achieving long-term success in managing ADHD symptoms through nutrition and physical activity.

Chapter 7: Sleep and Relaxation

7.1. The Importance of Sleep for ADHD Management

Sleep plays a critical role in ADHD management, as it directly impacts brain function, mood, and overall well-being. In this section, we will discuss the importance of sleep for individuals with ADHD and how it contributes to effective symptom management.

1. Brain function and cognition: During sleep, the brain undergoes essential processes such as memory consolidation, neural repair, and the removal of waste products. Adequate sleep supports optimal cognitive function, which is particularly important for individuals with ADHD who may struggle with attention, focus, and memory.

2. Emotional regulation: Sleep is crucial for emotional regulation, as it helps to balance neurotransmitters and hormones that impact mood. Insufficient sleep can exacerbate emotional difficulties often associated with ADHD, such as irritability, anxiety, and depression.

3. Impulse control and decision-making: Sleep deprivation can negatively affect the brain's prefrontal cortex, which is responsible for executive functions like impulse control and decision-making. Adequate sleep is essential for individuals with ADHD to effectively manage these aspects of their condition.

4. Physical health: Sleep plays a vital role in maintaining overall physical health by supporting immune function, cellular repair, and hormone regulation. Poor sleep can

contribute to a variety of health issues, such as obesity, diabetes, and cardiovascular disease, which can further complicate ADHD management.

5. Energy and motivation: Sufficient sleep helps to regulate energy levels and combat fatigue, which is crucial for individuals with ADHD who may struggle with motivation and productivity throughout the day.

6. Sleep disorders and ADHD: Individuals with ADHD are more likely to experience sleep disorders such as insomnia, sleep apnea, and restless leg syndrome. Proper sleep hygiene and professional help, when needed, can improve sleep quality and contribute to more effective ADHD management.

Given the critical role that sleep plays in ADHD management, it is essential for individuals with ADHD to prioritize healthy sleep habits and seek professional help if they experience ongoing sleep difficulties. By ensuring adequate and restorative sleep, individuals with ADHD can support optimal brain function, emotional regulation, and overall well-being, contributing to more effective symptom management.

7.2. Strategies for Improving Sleep Hygiene

Improving sleep hygiene involves adopting habits that promote restorative sleep and support overall well-being. In this section, we will provide practical strategies for individuals with ADHD to improve their sleep hygiene and achieve better sleep quality.

1. Establish a consistent sleep schedule: Go to bed and wake up at the same time every day, even on weekends. This helps regulate your body's internal clock and promotes better sleep quality.

2. Create a bedtime routine: Develop a relaxing pre-sleep routine to signal your body that it's time to wind down. This might include activities such as reading, taking a warm bath, or practicing gentle stretching or meditation.

3. Optimize your sleep environment: Make your bedroom a comfortable, quiet, and dark space conducive to sleep. Consider using blackout curtains, white noise machines, or earplugs to minimize disruptions. Keep the room temperature cool, ideally between 60-67°F (15-19°C).

4. Limit screen time before bed: Avoid electronic devices such as smartphones, tablets, and TVs for at least an hour before bedtime, as the blue light emitted by screens can interfere with the production of the sleep hormone melatonin.

5. Be mindful of caffeine and alcohol intake: Limit caffeine consumption to the earlier part of the day and avoid consuming alcohol close to bedtime, as both substances can disrupt sleep quality.

6. Exercise regularly: Engage in regular physical activity during the day, as this can help improve sleep quality. However, avoid vigorous exercise close to bedtime, as it may have a stimulating effect.

7. Manage stress and anxiety: Practice relaxation techniques, such as deep breathing, progressive muscle relaxation, or meditation, to help manage stress and anxiety that may interfere with sleep.

8. Limit daytime naps: If you're struggling with nighttime sleep, limit daytime naps to 20-30 minutes and avoid napping too close to bedtime.

9. Consider a light snack before bed: If you find yourself hungry before bedtime, opt for a light snack that combines complex carbohydrates and protein, such as whole-grain crackers with a slice of cheese or a small bowl of whole-grain cereal with milk.

10. Seek professional help if needed: If you continue to experience sleep difficulties despite implementing these strategies, consult with a healthcare professional or sleep specialist for further evaluation and guidance.

By following these sleep hygiene strategies, individuals with ADHD can improve their sleep quality and support more effective symptom management. Remember that achieving better sleep may take time and consistency, so be patient and persistent in your efforts to establish healthy sleep habits.

7.3. Relaxation Techniques for Better Sleep

Incorporating relaxation techniques into your daily routine and bedtime ritual can help reduce stress, calm the mind, and promote better sleep quality. In this section, we will discuss various relaxation techniques that individuals with ADHD can use to improve their sleep.

1. Deep breathing exercises: Focusing on slow, deep breaths can help activate the body's relaxation response. Practice diaphragmatic breathing by inhaling deeply through your nose, allowing your belly to expand, and then exhaling slowly through your mouth. Repeat this exercise for several minutes to promote relaxation.

2. Progressive muscle relaxation (PMR): PMR involves tensing and relaxing different muscle groups in a systematic order. Starting from your toes and moving up through your body, tense each muscle group for 5-10 seconds and then release the tension. This technique helps release physical tension and promotes overall relaxation.

3. Guided imagery: Guided imagery involves visualizing a peaceful, calming scene or environment in your mind. Close your eyes and imagine yourself in a relaxing setting, such as a beach or a serene forest. Focus on the details of the scene and engage all of your senses to deepen the relaxation experience.

4. Mindfulness meditation: Mindfulness meditation involves focusing your attention on the present moment and accepting it without judgment. Sit or lie down in a comfortable position and bring your attention to your

breath, bodily sensations, or a simple mantra. Gently redirect your focus to the present moment whenever your mind begins to wander.

5. Body scan meditation: During a body scan meditation, you'll mentally scan your body from head to toe, noticing any areas of tension or discomfort. As you become aware of these sensations, use your breath to help release the tension and promote relaxation.

6. Yoga and gentle stretching: Practicing gentle yoga or stretching exercises can help release physical tension and promote relaxation. Focus on slow, controlled movements and maintain a steady breath throughout the practice.

7. Aromatherapy: Using essential oils, such as lavender, chamomile, or valerian, can promote relaxation and improve sleep quality. Consider diffusing essential oils in your bedroom, applying them to your pulse points, or adding a few drops to a warm bath before bedtime.

8. Listen to calming music or nature sounds: Listening to soothing music or nature sounds can help create a relaxing atmosphere and facilitate sleep. Choose soft, slow-tempo music or calming sounds, such as rainfall or ocean waves.

9. Gratitude practice: Spend a few minutes reflecting on positive aspects of your day or things you are grateful for. This practice can help shift your focus away from stress and anxiety and promote a sense of relaxation and well-being.

10. Journaling: Writing down your thoughts, feelings, and

experiences can help clear your mind and reduce stress before bedtime. Consider dedicating a few minutes each night to writing in a journal as a part of your relaxation routine.

By incorporating these relaxation techniques into your daily routine and bedtime ritual, individuals with ADHD can promote better sleep quality and support more effective symptom management. Remember that it may take time to see improvements in sleep, so be patient and persistent in practicing relaxation techniques.

7.4. Managing ADHD-related Sleep Issues

Individuals with ADHD often experience sleep issues that can exacerbate their symptoms and impact overall well-being. In this section, we will discuss strategies for managing ADHD-related sleep issues and improving sleep quality.

1. Address sleep disorders: People with ADHD are more prone to sleep disorders such as insomnia, sleep apnea, and restless legs syndrome. Consult with a healthcare professional or sleep specialist to address any underlying sleep disorders and receive appropriate treatment.

2. Adjust medication timing: Stimulant medications used to treat ADHD can interfere with sleep if taken too late in the day. Talk to your healthcare provider about adjusting the timing of your medication to minimize sleep disruptions.

3. Create an ADHD-friendly bedtime routine: Establish a calming bedtime routine that accommodates your ADHD symptoms. This may involve incorporating additional relaxation techniques, using visual cues or reminders to stay on track, or setting aside extra time for winding down.

4. Manage nighttime hyperactivity: If you experience increased energy or hyperactivity at night, engage in calming activities before bedtime, such as reading, listening to soothing music, or practicing gentle stretching exercises. Avoid stimulating activities, such as vigorous exercise, video games, or screen time close to bedtime.

5. Limit exposure to blue light: As people with ADHD can be particularly sensitive to the effects of blue light, take extra precautions to minimize exposure to electronic screens in the evening. Consider using blue light-blocking glasses, screen filters, or apps that reduce blue light emissions.

6. Use a white noise machine or earplugs: If you are easily disturbed by noises during sleep, consider using a white noise machine or earplugs to block out potential distractions and promote a more restful sleep environment.

7. Practice cognitive behavioral techniques: Cognitive behavioral therapy (CBT) techniques can help address negative thoughts and behaviors that contribute to sleep difficulties. Consider working with a therapist or using self-help resources to learn and implement CBT strategies for improving sleep.

8. Implement a consistent daily schedule: Maintaining a consistent daily schedule, including regular mealtimes, exercise, and other activities, can help regulate your body's internal clock and promote better sleep quality.

9. Manage stress and anxiety: Chronic stress and anxiety can exacerbate sleep difficulties in individuals with ADHD. Implement stress-reduction techniques, such as mindfulness practices, deep breathing exercises, or journaling, to manage stress and promote relaxation.

10. Seek professional help: If you continue to experience sleep issues despite implementing these strategies, consult with a healthcare professional or sleep specialist

for further evaluation and guidance.

By addressing ADHD-related sleep issues and implementing strategies to improve sleep quality, individuals with ADHD can support more effective symptom management and enhance overall well-being. It's essential to be patient and persistent in your efforts to establish healthy sleep habits, as improvements in sleep may take time to achieve.

7.5. Creating a Bedtime Routine

Establishing a consistent bedtime routine can help signal to your body that it's time to wind down and prepare for sleep. In this section, we will discuss how individuals with ADHD can create a bedtime routine that promotes relaxation and improves sleep quality.

1. Set a consistent bedtime: Choose a bedtime that allows for an adequate amount of sleep (typically 7-9 hours for adults) and stick to it every night, even on weekends. Consistency helps regulate your body's internal clock and improves sleep quality.

2. Wind down gradually: Begin your bedtime routine about an hour before your intended sleep time. Gradually transition from more stimulating activities to calming ones to help your body and mind prepare for sleep.

3. Incorporate relaxation techniques: Include relaxation techniques such as deep breathing, progressive muscle relaxation, or mindfulness meditation as part of your bedtime routine to help reduce stress and create a sense of calm.

4. Engage in calming activities: Choose activities that help you unwind and relax, such as reading a book, taking a warm bath, or listening to soothing music or nature sounds.

5. Limit screen time: Avoid electronic devices such as smartphones, tablets, and TVs for at least an hour before bedtime. The blue light emitted by screens can interfere with the production of the sleep hormone melatonin.

6. Prepare your sleep environment: Ensure your bedroom is a comfortable, quiet, and dark space conducive to sleep. Adjust the room temperature, minimize noise and light, and create a comfortable and supportive sleep surface.

7. Practice gratitude or journaling: Reflect on positive aspects of your day or write down your thoughts and feelings in a journal to help clear your mind and promote relaxation.

8. Establish a pre-sleep hygiene routine: Engage in activities that signal to your body that it's time to prepare for sleep, such as brushing your teeth, washing your face, and changing into comfortable sleepwear.

9. Use visual reminders or cues: If you struggle to stay on track with your bedtime routine due to ADHD symptoms, consider using visual reminders or cues, such as a written checklist or timer, to help guide you through the routine.

10. Be flexible and adaptable: Your bedtime routine may need adjustments over time, so be open to making changes as needed. If a particular activity or technique isn't working for you, try something new and evaluate its effectiveness.

By creating a consistent bedtime routine that promotes relaxation and prepares your body for sleep, individuals with ADHD can improve sleep quality and support more effective symptom management. Remember that it may take time and patience to establish a routine that works best for you, so be persistent and flexible in your efforts to create a bedtime routine that supports your sleep needs.

Chapter 8: Medication and Therapy

8.1. An Overview of ADHD Medications

Medication is often a key component in the management of ADHD symptoms for many individuals. In this section, we will provide an overview of the different types of ADHD medications and their potential benefits and side effects.

1. Stimulant medications: Stimulant medications are the most commonly prescribed medications for ADHD. They work by increasing the levels of dopamine and norepinephrine in the brain, which helps improve focus, attention, and impulse control. There are two main types of stimulant medications:

a. Methylphenidate-based medications: Examples include Ritalin, Concerta, and Daytrana. These medications have a shorter duration of action and may need to be taken multiple times a day.

b. Amphetamine-based medications: Examples include Adderall, Vyvanse, and Dexedrine. These medications typically have a longer duration of action and may require fewer doses throughout the day.

2. Non-stimulant medications: Non-stimulant medications can also be used to treat ADHD, particularly for individuals who do not respond well to or cannot tolerate stimulant medications. Some examples of non-stimulant medications include:

a. Atomoxetine (Strattera): This medication works by

increasing the levels of norepinephrine in the brain, improving focus and attention. It has a longer duration of action and is taken once or twice a day.

b. Guanfacine (Intuniv) and Clonidine (Kapvay): These medications are alpha-2 adrenergic agonists and can help with impulse control and hyperactivity. They are often used in combination with stimulant medications to enhance their effectiveness.

It's essential to note that each individual's response to medication varies, and finding the right medication and dosage may require trial and error. Work closely with your healthcare provider to monitor your symptoms, side effects, and overall progress.

Potential side effects of ADHD medications may include:

- Appetite suppression and weight loss
- Sleep disturbances or insomnia
- Increased heart rate and blood pressure
- Nausea or stomach upset
- Headaches
- Mood changes or irritability

Most side effects are mild and tend to improve over time. However, if you experience severe or persistent side effects, consult with your healthcare provider to discuss potential adjustments to your medication or alternative treatment options.

In addition to medication, it's important to consider other treatment approaches, such as therapy, behavioral interventions, and lifestyle modifications, to effectively manage ADHD symptoms. The combination of medication and therapy often leads to the most significant improvements in ADHD management.

8.2. Navigating the Decision to Use Medication

Deciding whether or not to use medication for ADHD can be a challenging and complex process. In this section, we will discuss factors to consider when navigating the decision to use medication and strategies for making an informed choice.

1. Assess the severity of symptoms: Consider how ADHD symptoms impact your daily life, including school or work performance, relationships, and overall well-being. If symptoms are significantly interfering with your functioning and quality of life, medication may be a beneficial option.

2. Evaluate previous interventions: Reflect on the effectiveness of non-pharmacological interventions you have tried, such as therapy, coaching, or lifestyle modifications. If these approaches have not provided sufficient symptom relief, medication may be worth considering.

3. Consult with a healthcare professional: Discuss your concerns and symptoms with a healthcare professional experienced in diagnosing and treating ADHD. They can provide guidance on whether medication may be an appropriate treatment option and help you weigh the potential benefits and risks.

4. Research medication options: Educate yourself about the different types of ADHD medications, their potential benefits, and possible side effects. This will help you make an informed decision and facilitate discussions with your healthcare provider.

5. Consider personal factors: Reflect on your personal values, preferences, and medical history when making the decision to use medication. Factors such as personal beliefs about medication, potential drug interactions, or a history of substance abuse may influence your decision.

6. Involve family members or support systems: Engage your family members or close support systems in the decision-making process. Their input can provide valuable insights and help you consider different perspectives.

7. Be open to change: Recognize that the decision to use medication is not necessarily permanent. If you decide to try medication and find it is not effective or has intolerable side effects, you can always work with your healthcare provider to explore alternative treatments.

8. Monitor progress: Once you start medication, collaborate with your healthcare provider to closely monitor your symptoms, side effects, and overall progress. This will help you determine whether the medication is effective and make any necessary adjustments to dosage or type of medication.

9. Combine medication with other treatments: Keep in mind that medication is often most effective when combined with other interventions, such as therapy, behavioral strategies, and lifestyle modifications. Incorporate a comprehensive treatment approach to maximize symptom management.

10. Be patient: Finding the right medication and dosage may require trial and error. Be patient with the process

and communicate openly with your healthcare provider to find the most effective treatment for your unique needs.

Navigating the decision to use medication for ADHD can be a complex and personal journey. By considering these factors and working closely with a healthcare professional, you can make an informed decision that best supports your needs and helps you effectively manage ADHD symptoms.

8.3. The Role of Therapy in ADHD Management

Therapy plays a crucial role in ADHD management, as it can help individuals develop coping strategies, improve emotional regulation, and enhance overall functioning. In this section, we will discuss different types of therapy commonly used in ADHD management and their potential benefits.

1. Cognitive-Behavioral Therapy (CBT): CBT is a short-term, goal-oriented therapy that focuses on identifying and modifying unhelpful thought patterns and behaviors. It can help individuals with ADHD develop problem-solving skills, improve time management, and increase self-awareness.

2. Behavior Therapy: Behavior therapy is particularly useful for children with ADHD and their parents. It focuses on reinforcing positive behaviors and discouraging negative ones through techniques such as reward systems, time-outs, and setting clear expectations.

3. Psychoeducation: Psychoeducation involves providing individuals with ADHD and their families with information about the disorder, its symptoms, and available treatments. This can help them better understand the condition and develop effective strategies to cope with challenges.

4. Family Therapy: Family therapy can help families affected by ADHD learn to communicate more effectively, resolve conflicts, and support each other in managing ADHD symptoms.

5. Social Skills Training: Social skills training can be beneficial for individuals with ADHD who struggle with social interactions. It focuses on teaching specific social skills, such as active listening, maintaining eye contact, and taking turns in conversation.

6. Coaching: ADHD coaching is a collaborative, goal-oriented process that helps individuals with ADHD develop strategies for managing their symptoms, such as organization, time management, and goal-setting. Coaches can provide support, encouragement, and accountability.

7. Mindfulness-Based Interventions: Mindfulness-based interventions, such as mindfulness-based cognitive therapy (MBCT) or mindfulness-based stress reduction (MBSR), can help individuals with ADHD develop greater self-awareness, emotional regulation, and focus.

8. Group Therapy: Group therapy provides individuals with ADHD the opportunity to connect with others who share similar experiences, learn from one another, and develop a supportive network.

Therapy can be an essential component of a comprehensive treatment plan for ADHD. By participating in therapy, individuals with ADHD can develop the skills and strategies necessary to manage their symptoms more effectively and improve their overall functioning. It is important to work with a qualified mental health professional who has experience treating ADHD to ensure that the therapy is tailored to your unique needs and goals.

8.4. Types of Therapy and Their Benefits

Various types of therapy can be beneficial for individuals with ADHD, each with its unique approach and potential benefits. In this section, we will outline the most common types of therapy used in ADHD management and discuss their advantages.

1. Cognitive-Behavioral Therapy (CBT): CBT focuses on identifying and modifying negative thought patterns and behaviors, helping individuals with ADHD develop problem-solving skills, improve time management, and increase self-awareness. Benefits of CBT include enhanced emotional regulation, increased self-efficacy, and improved daily functioning.

2. Behavior Therapy: Behavior therapy is particularly useful for children with ADHD and their parents, as it emphasizes reinforcing positive behaviors and discouraging negative ones. Benefits include improved behavior at home and school, better parent-child communication, and increased self-esteem.

3. Psychoeducation: Psychoeducation provides individuals with ADHD and their families with information about the disorder, its symptoms, and available treatments. This can help increase understanding, reduce stigma, and promote the development of effective coping strategies.

4. Family Therapy: Family therapy can help families affected by ADHD learn to communicate more effectively, resolve conflicts, and support each other in managing ADHD symptoms. Benefits include improved family dynamics, increased understanding and empathy, and

strengthened family bonds.

5. Social Skills Training: Social skills training can be beneficial for individuals with ADHD who struggle with social interactions. This type of therapy focuses on teaching specific social skills, leading to improved relationships, increased self-confidence, and better communication abilities.

6. Coaching: ADHD coaching is a goal-oriented process that helps individuals with ADHD develop strategies for managing their symptoms. Benefits include enhanced organization, time management, and goal-setting, leading to improved daily functioning and increased self-esteem.

7. Mindfulness-Based Interventions: Mindfulness-based interventions can help individuals with ADHD develop greater self-awareness, emotional regulation, and focus. Benefits include reduced stress and anxiety, improved attention and concentration, and enhanced emotional well-being.

8. Group Therapy: Group therapy provides individuals with ADHD the opportunity to connect with others who share similar experiences, learn from one another, and develop a supportive network. Benefits include increased social support, reduced feelings of isolation, and the opportunity to learn new coping strategies from peers.

Selecting the right type of therapy depends on the individual's unique needs, preferences, and goals. By working with a qualified mental health professional experienced in treating ADHD, individuals can develop a tailored treatment plan that incorporates the most appropriate therapeutic approaches to effectively manage their symptoms and enhance their overall well-being.

8.5. Finding the Right Professional Support

Finding the right professional support for ADHD management is crucial to ensure the best possible outcome. In this section, we will discuss the steps to take and factors to consider when searching for the right mental health professional or ADHD specialist.

1. Identify your needs: Before seeking professional help, take the time to identify your specific needs and goals. This may include addressing ADHD symptoms, improving emotional regulation, enhancing social skills, or refining time management techniques.

2. Gather recommendations: Ask friends, family members, or healthcare providers for recommendations of professionals experienced in diagnosing and treating ADHD. You can also search online directories or contact professional organizations, such as the American Psychological Association, for referrals.

3. Research credentials and experience: Look for professionals who have the appropriate credentials, such as a licensed psychologist, psychiatrist, or clinical social worker, and who have experience treating individuals with ADHD.

4. Consider the professional's approach: Different professionals may use various treatment approaches, such as cognitive-behavioral therapy, behavior therapy, or medication management. Make sure to find a professional whose approach aligns with your needs and preferences.

5. Schedule a consultation: Arrange a consultation with

potential professionals to discuss your concerns, ask questions, and determine if their expertise and approach are a good fit for your needs.

6. Assess the rapport: Establishing a strong therapeutic relationship is essential for successful treatment. Pay attention to how comfortable you feel with the professional during your consultation, and whether you believe you can build trust and openly communicate with them.

7. Consider practical factors: Keep in mind logistical factors, such as the professional's location, availability, and whether they accept your insurance, as these can significantly impact your treatment experience.

8. Be open to change: If, after starting treatment, you feel that your chosen professional is not a good fit, it is okay to consider other options. Finding the right support may require some trial and error, but it is essential for successful ADHD management.

By taking these steps and considering these factors, you can find the right professional support to help you effectively manage ADHD symptoms and improve your overall well-being. Remember that building a strong therapeutic relationship and finding the best treatment approach for your unique needs are key components of successful ADHD management.

Chapter 9: Building Support Networks

9.1. The Importance of Social Support

Social support plays a crucial role in managing ADHD and maintaining overall well-being. In this section, we will discuss the importance of social support for individuals with ADHD and the various benefits it provides.

1. Emotional support: Having a strong support network allows individuals with ADHD to share their feelings, concerns, and experiences with understanding and empathetic listeners. This can provide a sense of comfort, reduce feelings of isolation, and help process emotions more effectively.

2. Practical assistance: Friends, family members, and other supportive individuals can provide practical assistance, such as helping with time management, organization, or decision-making. This support can alleviate stress and help individuals with ADHD manage their symptoms more effectively.

3. Accountability: A supportive network can encourage individuals with ADHD to stay committed to their goals, whether related to treatment, personal growth, or daily tasks. Supportive individuals can help keep them accountable and motivated to continue working towards their objectives.

4. Encouragement and validation: Supportive people can provide encouragement and validation, helping individuals with ADHD to recognize their strengths, accomplishments, and progress. This can boost self-

esteem and promote a more positive self-image.

5. Sharing coping strategies: Connecting with others who have ADHD or similar experiences can provide valuable insights and tips for managing symptoms. By sharing coping strategies, individuals with ADHD can learn new techniques and perspectives to better manage their condition.

6. Reducing stigma: A strong support network can help challenge misconceptions and stigma surrounding ADHD, promoting a greater understanding and acceptance of the condition.

7. Enhancing resilience: Social support can play a crucial role in developing emotional resilience, helping individuals with ADHD to better cope with challenges and setbacks.

Building a strong support network is an essential component of ADHD management, offering emotional, practical, and motivational benefits that can contribute to improved well-being and more effective symptom management. By cultivating supportive relationships and connections, individuals with ADHD can enhance their resilience and better navigate the challenges associated with their condition.

9.2. Connecting with Others Who Have ADHD

Connecting with others who have ADHD can provide valuable support, understanding, and shared experiences, making it easier to navigate the challenges associated with the condition. In this section, we will discuss various ways to connect with others who have ADHD and the potential benefits of these connections.

1. Support groups: Local and online ADHD support groups offer an opportunity for individuals to share their experiences, discuss coping strategies, and provide mutual encouragement. Many organizations, such as CHADD (Children and Adults with Attention-Deficit/ Hyperactivity Disorder), offer resources for finding ADHD support groups in your area or online.

2. Social media: Social media platforms, such as Facebook, Instagram, and Twitter, can be an excellent way to connect with others who have ADHD. Look for groups, pages, or hashtags related to ADHD, and engage with others who share similar experiences.

3. Online forums: Online forums dedicated to ADHD, such as ADDitude Magazine's online community or ADHD subreddit, provide a platform for individuals to ask questions, share experiences, and offer support to one another.

4. Workshops and conferences: Attend workshops, conferences, or seminars related to ADHD to meet others with the condition, as well as professionals in the field. These events can provide valuable networking opportunities and access to the latest information and resources.

5. Local events: Keep an eye out for local events related to ADHD, such as awareness walks or fundraisers, where you can connect with others who share your experiences and interests.

6. Friends and family: Open up to friends and family members about your ADHD diagnosis, as they may know others with the condition or have similar experiences themselves. Sharing your experiences can strengthen existing relationships and create new connections.

7. Therapy groups: Participating in therapy groups specifically designed for individuals with ADHD can provide an opportunity to connect with others who have the condition, while also working on personal growth and development.

Connecting with others who have ADHD can be an invaluable source of support, understanding, and camaraderie. By actively seeking out and engaging with others who share similar experiences, individuals with ADHD can build a supportive network that contributes to their overall well-being and more effective symptom management.

9.3. Establishing Healthy Relationships

Establishing healthy relationships is crucial for individuals with ADHD, as these connections can provide essential support and contribute to overall well-being. In this section, we will discuss strategies for building and maintaining healthy relationships, both with new acquaintances and existing friends and family members.

1. Communication: Open and honest communication is the foundation of any healthy relationship. Practice active listening, express your thoughts and feelings clearly, and be willing to engage in difficult conversations when necessary. This helps to build trust and understanding between you and your loved ones.

2. Empathy: Develop empathy by putting yourself in others' shoes and considering their feelings, experiences, and perspectives. Being empathetic and understanding can foster a strong emotional connection and help others feel valued and supported.

3. Set boundaries: Establish clear boundaries to maintain a balance between your needs and those of others. Communicate your limits and expectations, and respect the boundaries of others as well.

4. Be reliable: Show up for others when you say you will, and follow through on your commitments. Being reliable and dependable helps to build trust in your relationships.

5. Support each other: Offer your support to friends and family members, and be open to receiving support from them as well. A strong support network can be a source of

comfort and encouragement during challenging times.

6. Practice patience: ADHD can sometimes lead to impulsive behavior or difficulties with time management. Be patient with yourself and others, and understand that everyone makes mistakes and faces challenges.

7. Engage in shared activities: Participate in activities that both you and your friends or family members enjoy. Shared interests can strengthen your bond and provide opportunities for positive interaction.

8. Foster personal growth: Encourage your friends and family members to pursue their goals and aspirations, and seek their support in your own personal growth journey. Healthy relationships enable individuals to grow and evolve together.

9. Address conflicts constructively: Conflicts are a natural part of any relationship. Approach disagreements with respect, and work together to find solutions that address everyone's needs and concerns.

10. Appreciate and celebrate: Show appreciation for the support and love you receive from others, and celebrate your achievements and milestones together. This helps to build a positive and nurturing environment in your relationships.

By implementing these strategies, individuals with ADHD can establish and maintain healthy relationships that provide essential support, understanding, and encouragement, contributing to their overall well-being and more effective symptom management.

9.4. Communicating Effectively with Loved Ones

Effective communication is key to maintaining healthy relationships and ensuring that your loved ones understand your ADHD-related needs and experiences. In this section, we will discuss strategies for communicating effectively with friends and family members, which can foster greater understanding and support.

1. Be open and honest: Share your feelings, experiences, and challenges related to ADHD with your loved ones. By being open and honest, you can help them better understand your needs and the impact of ADHD on your life.

2. Choose the right time and place: Select an appropriate setting for important conversations, free from distractions and interruptions. This will help to create a comfortable environment for open and focused discussions.

3. Use "I" statements: Express your thoughts and feelings using "I" statements, such as "I feel overwhelmed when..." or "I need help with..." This helps to promote understanding and prevents others from feeling blamed or attacked.

4. Actively listen: Pay attention to what your loved ones are saying, and demonstrate that you are listening by nodding, maintaining eye contact, and asking follow-up questions. Active listening helps to build trust and fosters open communication.

5. Be patient: Understand that your loved ones may not

immediately grasp the challenges you face due to ADHD. Be patient as you explain your experiences and answer their questions.

6. Offer solutions: When discussing challenges or difficulties, try to present potential solutions or strategies that you believe may help. This shows that you are proactive in addressing your needs and encourages collaboration.

7. Encourage questions: Invite your loved ones to ask questions about ADHD and your experiences. This can help to create a deeper understanding and ensure that everyone is on the same page.

8. Show appreciation: Express gratitude for your loved ones' support, understanding, and willingness to learn about ADHD. This can help to strengthen your relationships and encourage continued support.

9. Keep the lines of communication open: Regularly check in with your loved ones to discuss your ADHD-related needs, progress, and any new challenges that may arise. Maintaining open communication can help to ensure ongoing understanding and support.

By implementing these strategies, individuals with ADHD can effectively communicate with their loved ones, fostering greater understanding, support, and collaboration in managing the challenges associated with the condition.

9.5. Finding Support Groups and Resources

Support groups and resources can provide invaluable assistance for individuals with ADHD, offering a sense of community, understanding, and shared experiences. In this section, we will discuss how to find support groups and resources tailored to ADHD, which can help you build connections and access information to better manage your symptoms.

1. Local support groups: Many communities have local support groups for individuals with ADHD and their families. These groups typically hold regular meetings and provide an opportunity to share experiences, ask questions, and learn from one another. To find a local support group, check with your healthcare provider, community centers, or mental health organizations.

2. Online support groups: In addition to local support groups, there are numerous online forums and communities dedicated to ADHD. These platforms, such as ADDitude Magazine's online community or ADHD subreddit, allow individuals to connect with others who have ADHD from around the world. This can be particularly helpful for those who may not have access to local support groups or prefer the anonymity of online discussions.

3. Nonprofit organizations: Many nonprofit organizations, such as CHADD (Children and Adults with Attention-Deficit/Hyperactivity Disorder), provide resources and support for individuals with ADHD and their families. These organizations often offer local and online support groups, workshops, and educational materials.

4. Social media: Social media platforms, such as Facebook, Instagram, and Twitter, can be useful for connecting with others who have ADHD and finding support groups or resources. Look for groups, pages, or hashtags related to ADHD, and engage with others who share similar experiences.

5. Workshops and conferences: Attending workshops, conferences, or seminars related to ADHD can help you connect with others who have the condition and provide access to the latest information, resources, and professional support. Many organizations offer events specifically tailored to ADHD, which can be a valuable source of connection and education.

6. Mental health professionals: Your healthcare provider or mental health professional may be able to recommend support groups, resources, or other services tailored to ADHD. Don't hesitate to ask for their guidance in finding the support you need.

7. Educational institutions: If you are a student or have a child with ADHD, your school or university may offer support groups or resources for students with ADHD. Reach out to the school's counseling or disability services department for information about available resources.

By exploring these options and connecting with others who have ADHD, you can build a strong support network that contributes to your overall well-being and more effective symptom management. Taking advantage of available resources can help you better understand and navigate the challenges associated with ADHD, ultimately leading to greater success and fulfillment.

Chapter 10: Advocacy and Empowerment

10.1. Understanding Your Rights as an Individual with ADHD

Understanding your rights as an individual with ADHD is essential to advocate for yourself and ensure that you receive the support and accommodations you need to succeed. In this section, we will discuss the various rights and protections afforded to individuals with ADHD and how you can become informed and empowered to advocate for yourself.

1. Disability rights and anti-discrimination laws: ADHD is recognized as a disability under various laws, such as the Americans with Disabilities Act (ADA) in the United States, and similar legislation in other countries. These laws protect individuals with ADHD from discrimination in areas such as employment, education, and public services, and require reasonable accommodations to be provided as needed.

2. Educational rights: In educational settings, students with ADHD may be eligible for accommodations and support services under laws such as the Individuals with Disabilities Education Act (IDEA) in the United States, and equivalent laws in other countries. These protections may include Individualized Education Plans (IEPs) or Section 504 plans, which outline specific accommodations and support services to help students succeed academically.

3. Workplace rights: Employees with ADHD have the right to request reasonable accommodations in the workplace,

such as a flexible work schedule, a quieter workspace, or additional breaks. Employers are required by law to provide these accommodations unless they pose an undue hardship on the business.

4. Confidentiality: Your ADHD diagnosis is considered personal medical information, and you have the right to keep it confidential. Employers, educational institutions, and service providers are generally not allowed to disclose your ADHD diagnosis without your consent, except in specific circumstances outlined by law.

5. Access to services and support: As an individual with ADHD, you have the right to access services and support, such as therapy, medication, or counseling, which can help you manage your symptoms and lead a fulfilling life.

To advocate for your rights and empower yourself as an individual with ADHD:

1. Educate yourself: Learn about the laws and protections in your country that apply to individuals with ADHD. Familiarize yourself with the specific rights and accommodations that you are entitled to in educational, workplace, and public settings.

2. Document your needs: Keep records of your ADHD diagnosis, any evaluations or assessments, and documentation of the accommodations you require. This information will be important when requesting accommodations or advocating for your rights.

3. Speak up: If you believe that your rights are being violated or you are not receiving the accommodations you

need, speak up and advocate for yourself. Communicate your needs clearly and assertively, and provide documentation to support your requests.

4. Seek support: Reach out to support groups, mental health professionals, or advocacy organizations for guidance and assistance in advocating for your rights. They can provide valuable resources, advice, and support in navigating the process.

5. Educate others: Share your experiences with ADHD and educate others about the condition. By raising awareness and understanding, you can help to reduce stigma and create a more inclusive environment for individuals with ADHD.

Understanding and advocating for your rights as an individual with ADHD is crucial to ensuring that you receive the support and accommodations necessary for success in all areas of life. By becoming informed and empowered, you can take control of your ADHD journey and work towards a fulfilling, successful future.

10.2. Advocating for Accommodations at Work and School

Successfully advocating for accommodations in work and school settings is essential for individuals with ADHD to optimize their performance and well-being. In this section, we will discuss strategies for effectively advocating for the accommodations you need in both work and educational environments.

1. Know your rights: Familiarize yourself with the laws and protections that apply to individuals with ADHD in your country, such as the Americans with Disabilities Act (ADA) or the Individuals with Disabilities Education Act (IDEA) in the United States. Understanding your rights is crucial for advocating effectively.

2. Gather documentation: Prepare documentation of your ADHD diagnosis, including any evaluations or assessments, and a list of accommodations that you require. This information will be necessary when requesting accommodations from employers or educational institutions.

3. Develop a clear request: Clearly outline the specific accommodations you need, and explain how they will help you succeed in your work or academic setting. Be prepared to provide examples and evidence to support your request.

4. Schedule a meeting: Request a meeting with your supervisor, human resources department, or school administrators to discuss your needs and present your request for accommodations. Choose a time and place that is conducive to a focused, private conversation.

5. Be proactive and solution-focused: During the meeting, present your request in a proactive and solution-focused manner. Explain the benefits of the accommodations, not only for yourself but also for the organization or school. Offer to collaborate on finding solutions that work for both parties.

6. Follow up in writing: After your meeting, send a written summary of your request and any agreed-upon accommodations. This documentation can serve as a reference for both parties and help to ensure that the accommodations are implemented as agreed.

7. Monitor progress and communicate: Regularly assess the effectiveness of the accommodations and communicate any necessary adjustments with your employer or school. Open communication and collaboration are key to ensuring that the accommodations remain effective over time.

8. Know when to seek additional support: If you encounter resistance or feel that your rights are not being respected, seek guidance from advocacy organizations, legal resources, or mental health professionals. They can provide support and advice on navigating challenging situations and advocating for your rights.

By effectively advocating for accommodations at work and school, individuals with ADHD can create an environment that supports their success and well-being. Proactively addressing your needs and collaborating with employers and educators can lead to a more inclusive and understanding environment, ultimately benefiting all parties involved.

10.3. Raising Awareness and Reducing Stigma

Raising awareness and reducing stigma surrounding ADHD is vital for fostering a more inclusive and understanding society. In this section, we will discuss strategies for increasing awareness about ADHD and challenging misconceptions that contribute to the stigma associated with the condition.

1. Share your story: One of the most powerful ways to raise awareness and reduce stigma is by sharing your personal experiences with ADHD. By discussing your journey, you can provide insight into the realities of living with ADHD and challenge misconceptions that others may have.

2. Educate others: Take the initiative to educate friends, family, coworkers, and educators about ADHD. Share facts, dispel myths, and provide information about the condition to help others develop a more accurate understanding of what it means to live with ADHD.

3. Use social media: Utilize social media platforms to share information, resources, and personal experiences related to ADHD. By joining online conversations and sharing your perspective, you can reach a wider audience and contribute to a more informed and empathetic understanding of the condition.

4. Participate in awareness events: Get involved in ADHD awareness events, such as conferences, workshops, webinars, or awareness days. By participating in these events, you can learn more about the condition and connect with others who share your experiences.

5. Volunteer with advocacy organizations: Offer your time and skills to support nonprofit organizations that advocate for individuals with ADHD. By working with these organizations, you can contribute to their mission and help raise awareness about the condition on a larger scale.

6. Encourage media representation: Support and promote accurate media representation of ADHD by endorsing TV shows, movies, books, and articles that portray the condition authentically. Encourage media outlets to consult with individuals who have ADHD or mental health experts to ensure that their portrayals are accurate and sensitive.

7. Challenge stereotypes: When you encounter stereotypes or misconceptions about ADHD, address them directly and provide accurate information to counter these beliefs. By challenging stereotypes, you can contribute to a more informed and understanding society.

8. Foster a supportive environment: Encourage open dialogue about ADHD in your social circles, workplace, and educational settings. By creating a supportive and inclusive environment, you can help reduce the stigma associated with ADHD and promote understanding among those around you.

By actively raising awareness and reducing stigma surrounding ADHD, individuals and communities can foster a more inclusive and understanding society. Through education, open dialogue, and challenging misconceptions, we can work together to support and empower individuals with ADHD and promote their success and well-being.

10.4. Becoming an Active Participant in Your Treatment Plan

Becoming an active participant in your ADHD treatment plan is crucial for achieving long-term success and personal growth. In this section, we will discuss strategies for effectively engaging in your treatment plan and collaborating with professionals to manage your ADHD symptoms.

1. Educate yourself: Learn as much as you can about ADHD, including its causes, symptoms, and potential treatments. Understanding the condition will empower you to make informed decisions about your treatment and help you advocate for your needs.

2. Establish open communication: Develop a strong, open line of communication with your healthcare providers, therapists, and other professionals involved in your treatment. Share your experiences, concerns, and preferences with them to ensure that your treatment plan is tailored to your unique needs and circumstances.

3. Set realistic goals: Work with your healthcare team to establish clear, achievable goals for your treatment. These goals should be specific, measurable, and time-bound, and should reflect your personal values and priorities.

4. Track your progress: Keep a journal or use a tracking app to monitor your symptoms, medication effects, and progress toward your treatment goals. Regularly review this information with your healthcare team to assess the effectiveness of your treatment plan and make any necessary adjustments.

5. Be proactive in seeking support: Reach out to support groups, mental health professionals, and advocacy organizations for guidance and assistance in managing your ADHD. They can provide valuable resources, advice, and support to help you navigate the challenges of living with ADHD.

6. Advocate for your needs: Speak up when you feel that your treatment plan is not addressing your needs or when you believe that alternative approaches should be considered. Your healthcare team should be receptive to your input and willing to explore different options to find the best fit for you.

7. Collaborate with your healthcare team: Actively engage in the decision-making process and collaborate with your healthcare team to develop a treatment plan that is tailored to your needs. By taking an active role in your treatment, you can help ensure that your plan is effective and sustainable over time.

8. Practice self-care: Prioritize self-care by addressing your physical, mental, and emotional well-being. Develop healthy habits, such as regular exercise, a balanced diet, and consistent sleep routines, to support your overall health and the success of your treatment plan.

By becoming an active participant in your treatment plan, you can take control of your ADHD journey and work collaboratively with your healthcare team to manage your symptoms effectively. Through proactive engagement and self-advocacy, you can optimize your treatment plan and pave the way for personal growth and success.

10.5. Embracing Your ADHD Identity and Using It to Empower Yourself

Embracing your ADHD identity is a vital step in empowering yourself and achieving personal success. Recognizing the unique strengths and qualities that ADHD brings to your life can help you build self-confidence and resilience. In this section, we will discuss strategies for embracing your ADHD identity and using it to empower yourself.

1. Accept and embrace your diagnosis: Recognize that ADHD is a part of who you are, and accept it without shame or self-judgment. Understand that ADHD comes with both challenges and strengths, and that your unique experiences and perspectives can enrich your life.

2. Focus on your strengths: Identify your strengths and talents that are related to your ADHD, such as creativity, out-of-the-box thinking, hyperfocus, or spontaneity. Celebrate these strengths and incorporate them into your personal and professional life to maximize your potential.

3. Develop self-compassion: Treat yourself with kindness and understanding, acknowledging that living with ADHD can be challenging. Practice self-compassion by acknowledging your struggles and offering yourself the same support and encouragement you would give to a friend.

4. Reframe your perspective: Rather than viewing ADHD as a deficit or limitation, try to see it as a unique aspect of your identity that offers valuable skills and insights. By reframing your perspective, you can develop a more positive self-image and recognize the potential benefits of

living with ADHD.

5. Share your experiences: Openly discuss your ADHD journey with friends, family, and colleagues. Sharing your story can help to reduce stigma, foster understanding, and create opportunities for you to connect with others who share similar experiences.

6. Seek out role models: Find successful individuals with ADHD who inspire and motivate you. Learn from their stories, strategies, and accomplishments to help you navigate your own ADHD journey and empower yourself to reach your goals.

7. Set achievable goals: Establish realistic goals that align with your strengths and values. By setting achievable goals, you can build self-confidence and demonstrate to yourself and others that ADHD does not define your potential for success.

8. Advocate for yourself and others: Use your voice and experiences to advocate for yourself and others with ADHD. Raise awareness, challenge stereotypes, and work to create a more inclusive and understanding environment for individuals with ADHD.

9. Connect with the ADHD community: Join support groups, online forums, or attend conferences to connect with others who have ADHD. These connections can provide invaluable support, resources, and encouragement as you embrace your ADHD identity.

By embracing your ADHD identity and using it to empower yourself, you can cultivate self-confidence, resilience, and personal growth. Recognizing your unique strengths and experiences can help you to navigate the challenges of living with ADHD and unlock your full potential for success.

NOTES:

NOTES:

NOTES:

NOTES:

9 798393 653125